I CAN'T MAKE YOU LOVE HIM

~~~~~~~~~~~~~~~

Jolene McCall

I Can't Make You Love Him
Copyright © 2018 by Hori-Son Press
info@horisonpress.com

All rights reserved. No portion of this book may be reproduced, stored in a retrieval system, or transmitted in any form or by any means electronic, mechanical photocopy, recording, or any other except for brief quotations in printed reviews, without the prior permission of the Publisher or Copyright Owner.

Cover Design by Lynn H. Pellerin
Cover Photo by Karmin Jones

ISBN 978-1-938186-05-9

SAN 920-251X

Throughout this book, the name satan has deliberately not been capitalized. To capitalize a name would be proper grammar, and it also shows respect to that person. Since, I have no respect for satan or any demonic force of that nature, I choose to be grammatically incorrect and refrain from capitalizing his name.

"Scripture taken from the NEW AMERICAN STANDARD BIBLE®, Copyright © 1960, 1962, 1963, 1971, 1972, 1973, 1975, 1977, 1995 by The Lockman Foundation. Used by permission."

Scripture taken from the HOLY BIBLE, NEW INTERNATIONAL VERSION®. Copyright © 1973, 1978, 1984 Biblical. Used by permission of Zondervan. All rights reserved.

"Scripture taken from the New King James Version. Copyright © 1982 by Thomas Nelson, Inc. Used by permission. All rights reserved."

"Scripture quotations taken from the Amplified® Bible, Copyright © 1954, 1958, 1962, 1964, 1965, 1987 by The Lockman Foundation. Used by permission." (www.Lockman.org)

"Scripture quotations marked (ESV) are from The Holy Bible, English Standard Version® (ESV®), copyright © 2001 by Crossway, a publishing ministry of Good News Publishers. Used by permission. All rights reserved."

Scripture quotations from THE MESSAGE. Copyright © by Eugene H. Peterson 1993, 1994, 1995, 1996, 2000, 2001, 2002. Used by permission of NavPress. All rights reserved. Represented by Tyndale House Publishers, Inc.

Scripture quotations are taken from the Holy Bible, New Living Translation, copyright ©1996, 2004, 2007, 2013, 2015 by Tyndale House Foundation. Used by permission of Tyndale House Publishers, Inc., Carol Stream, Illinois 60188. All rights reserved.

Scriptures marked HCSB are taken from the HOLMAN CHRISTIAN STANDARD BIBLE (HCSB): Scripture taken from the HOLMAN CHRISTIAN STANDARD BIBLE, copyright© 1999, 2000, 2002, 2003 by Holman Bible Publishers, Nashville Tennessee. All rights reserved.

Public domain Bibles may be used freely, without restriction and without prior permission. The following Bibles in the English section of BibleGateway.com are in the public domain and can be used freely without restriction or prior permission from us or anyone else:

King James Version (Crown copyright/Public Domain in the United States)

American Standard Version (No copyright information is available)

New Life Version (No copyright information is available)

Weymouth New Testament Scripture quotations marked Weymouth are from the Weymouth New Testament, Richard Francis Weymouth, 1912. Public domain in the United States.

Acknowledgements

To my Heavenly Father,

I pray that my days are filled with your presence, that you sustain me in all things. Strengthen me Lord where I am weak and lead me not into waters that will overtake me but always be by my side that I grow in Your love, Your ways, Your wisdom and knowledge. Let the path I choose be one that brings You glory above all. This book Lord is Your book, and let it glorify Your name above all names with every word which is written and that my life be one of service unto You and Your plan.

Dedication

This book is dedicated to my first grandchild, Jerrika. Through the years I have raised you and loved you; God has been gracious to give me the tools needed at just the right time. I am thankful that your life has given me the healing I needed in order that God's grace has surrounded me, sustained me, and brought me to greater depths that I never knew were possible. I pray that these words within this book will always be a light unto your path and a lamp unto your feet.

Table of Contents

Acknowledgement v

Introduction xi

1 Life Minus God 1

2 As In The Days Of Noah 13

3 For The Least Of These 29

4 Loving From The Inside 49

5 I Can't Make You Love Him 57

6 Having Done All - Stand 63

7 Pioneers For Christ 71

Conclusion 87

References 89

INTRODUCTION

This book is for everyone as I believe we can never have too much Jesus! Years ago, going through a hard spell with my granddaughter that I had been raising, I began praying over her every single morning on the way to her school. Every day after praying myself, I would ask her if she also wanted to pray. Her reply was always, *"NO!"* One morning, as tears began to flow down my cheeks, silently, I spoke to God saying, *"Lord, I can't make her love You!"*

You see, I know that just being raised in church or in a family that believes in Jesus does NOT guarantee that you or your children will make it to Heaven. I knew that if I could not make her love Jesus, one day, she would walk away. If I could not instill enough Jesus in her, she would make the choice to fall away. God spoke to me that day and said, *"You can't make her love Me, and you can't even make yourself fall in love with Me!"*

Think of it like this, many people today get married because they feel the other person would be good for them, but they are not <u>IN LOVE</u> with them! Sometimes, we make the choice to be in a relationship for whatever reason but if truth be known, we may love the person because they are good to us, but we are NOT in love with that person. We cannot make ourselves fall in love with someone just because it is the right thing to do or because we know that person may be what is best for us.

So truthfully, none of us are capable of making ourselves fall in love with God no matter how hard we try. However, it is a start! You see, our love and God's love are two different things. We love conditional and God loves unconditional. Our love towards God normally begins with, *"What is in it for me?"* Sometimes the question sounds like this, *"God, I need You to fix my life; I need You to get me out of this mess; I need You to open the door for a job; I need this, or I need that!"* Sometimes, we can condition ourselves to love someone that is good for us, but we still cannot make ourselves FALL IN LOVE with them!

Love will be discussed extensively throughout this book but first, we need to know that God's love is totally different than the way the world loves. The closest we get to loving like God loves is when we have children. The Bible says that we love Him because He first loved us. Yes, He did love us first and this is the beginning to learn how to really fall in love with Him.

1 John 4:19 (KJV) [19]We love him, because he first loved us.

I'm quick to remind my grandchildren when they tell me they love me more than I love them that the Bible says that they cannot love me more. Of course, the older ones are quick to say, *"That's not in the Bible."* However, it is in the Bible. The Bible says that we love Him because He first loved us! Our children or grandchildren love us because we first loved them! So, the reason my grandchildren cannot love me more is because I loved them first! The love we have for our parents begins because they did love us first. If we were fortunate to grow up in a home where there was genuine love from parents *(two parents)* it becomes easier to grow to love God as well. However, the sad part is that the family unit has gradually been declining over the years where there are many parents missing from the home, many suffer from addictions, struggle to provide for their children, and many were not raised in a loving home to begin with. All of these areas produce negative consequences upon their children and the cycle continues. Then there are many homes today that do have two parents, but many have been so programmed to this world that the entertainment in society today plagues their lives. This would be all the modern technology that has crept into the family unit ultimately bringing destruction. Multitudes of parents today spend countless hours talking on their phones, texting, surfing the internet, overtime with their jobs to pay for all their luxuries, etc. All of these things keep the modern-day families conformed to this world, and the entertainment on the television has gradually become the normal which has allowed ungodliness to creep into most homes today. If we were to go back to the 60s, those things allowed to entertain our children today would have never been allowed in most homes. Not to forget, all the modern technology with video games that can be programmed to televisions, cell phones, etc. which have taken away valuable time and attention that parents could be spending with their children. You see just as many parents addicted to all the different elements of entertainment as you do children today where there is so much lacking within the parent-child relationships and husband-wife relationships. As I cried out to God that day, desiring that my granddaughter come to know Him and love Him, a journey began but not without confirmation.

As I spoke to God that morning, He told me on the way to her school, *"Speak a love letter to me!"* What did that mean? Going back to a time of young love, I could remember those years when you think you are so in love with someone and the love letters begin. Most of us can probably relate to that. All God was asking me to do was to read my love letter that was embedded in my mind to Him. He wanted me to speak it out. I could not make her love Him, but I could begin to learn how to express my love for God openly and ultimately fall deeper in love with Him myself. By doing so, this would allow her to experience what I was feeling for our God.

This was the beginning of radically changing my heart in a powerful way. Every morning from that point, I would tell her, *"I'm going to speak a love letter to Jesus"* and then I would begin. I would pray my love letter aloud. I would speak what I was feeling in my heart. I was learning to love Jesus more intimately as I expressed how great our Lord is because of all those things over the years He had brought me through. I was expressing those hidden things in my heart which I felt because I could remember a time in my life of darkness when my life was minus God. I could remember how alone I felt during those years. I could remember what it was like to be raised without love. I could remember being filled with sadness during several tragedies in my lifetime and then there was Jesus to pick up the pieces just because HE LOVED ME! After speaking my love letter, I would ask her, *"Would you like to speak your love letter to Him also?"* She began doing the same thing, and I began to see a change within her.

Our God is so good that He also gave me a confirmation on what He had asked me to do. The first day that He spoke to me to speak my love letter to Him, He also spoke to one of my daughters. She had called me that day and I was so excited to tell her about what had inspired, but she wasn't able to talk very long and was going to call me back. That day, I did not get to share it with her only to find out later that God was not ready for me to tell her. The following day, I went to lunch with that same daughter. After we sat down, I once again started to try and share with her what God had showed me only for her to jump in and say, *"I have to tell you what God showed me last night!"* So patiently, I listened to hear what God evidently wanted me to know before I shared with her my experience. The night prior, she was trying to spend time with God and many times when she would be going through things over the years, she would go to her piano and play. This had always been her escape and time to spend with God as she was growing up. As she began playing her piano, God spoke to her and said, *"Sing your love letter to Me!"* How awesome is our God! My daughter being a singer, her love letter would naturally come through her song but mine would come through my words since my gift was in writing.

All journeys traveled will lead to a destination and through this journey, our destination can be to know Him deeper, love Him more genuine, and forgive greater!

CHAPTER ONE
LIFE MINUS GOD

Like many of you who will stumble across this book, I was not raised in a home where Jesus was the center of our family. In fact, in my home growing up, there was no mention of anything to do with the Bible. However, even if homes do mention the Bible from time to time or go to church from time to time, it would probably be safe to say that most homes today do not really have Jesus in the midst. They may even go to church on a regular basis, but the point is, this generation has stepped back from living a holy life. Christianity today is not as it was in biblical days. In my own home growing up, we were not even raised knowing who God was or who Jesus was. I grew up not even understanding what the difference was between God and Jesus and not sure if I had ever even heard anyone speak of the Holy Spirit. Like most homes in America, ours was filled with the beliefs and perceptions of this world. In other words, we did not know anything about the Bible and lived just like everyone else in this world who live daily being conformed to this world instead of transformed by the Word of God! We were consumed with obtaining the American Dream.

Growing up in the 60's and 70's, I can remember that the American Dream was to be able to work hard enough so that you could own your own home, car, and live a life of comfort. However, your definition of the American Dream probably depended on how you were raised. Many people believed that obtaining the American Dream was much more than having materialism. To many it was about living a simple life but a happy fulfilled life.[1] America, being the land of the free, began the search for that freedom to obtain what could have never been obtained under the religious persecution and strict rules in England. As a result, the Bill of Rights was established and added to the Constitution which became the first ten amendments.

Our freedoms included the following:

Freedom of Religion
Freedom of Speech
Freedom of Press
Freedom of Assembly
Freedom of Petition
The Right to Bear Arms
"No-Quartering" Right
The Right to Equal Justice
The Right to Own Private Property
The Right to Enjoy Many Other Freedoms[2]

Due to America's Constitution, all citizens had freedoms and because of these freedoms, the American Dream could be obtained by the individual based on their own perspectives. In reality, the American Dream to most people especially today, is all about getting ahead in this world and being like everyone else who strives for this concept. All is good if you obtain an education, have a decent job in order to plan for your future, your children's future, and your retirement. This is all a dream that comes to an end eventually. When we reach the end of that plateau, what have we really accomplished? Your concept of the American Dream may be to live a simple life, striving for happiness; however, it can still be a life minus God. At the end of this road, we must ask ourselves if this life was about making a mark in this world, or about conforming to this world, or was it about preparing for the world to come? There are two Scriptures that should be our focus here.

Romans 12:2 (ESV) ²Do not be conformed to this world, but be transformed by the renewal of your mind, that by testing you may discern what is the will of God, what is good and acceptable and perfect.

John 17:6, 9, 16-17 (ESV) ⁶"I have manifested your name to the people whom you gave me out of the world. Yours they were, and you gave them to me, and they have kept your word. ⁹I am praying for them. <u>I am not praying for the world but for those whom you have given me</u>, for they are yours. ¹⁶<u>They are not of the world, just as I am not of the world</u>. ¹⁷Sanctify them in the truth; your word is truth.

It would be to your advantage to read John 17 in full, but I wanted to clarify that Jesus is praying for those who are His. Just because we claim to be Christians does not make us a Christian. Jesus tells us that those who belong to Him are no more of this world than He is of this world. If we claim to be Christians today, our lives must portray Jesus Christ living in and through us. Jesus was never about trying to be conformed to this world. He lived and breathed a life which was all about His Father. His life lives on today because He made an impact on this world and those first disciples also made an impact. There has never been anyone nor will there ever be anyone whose life has or will live on like that of Jesus Christ. Those disciples of Jesus Christ which we read about in the Bible, their lives live on to impact our lives today only because their focus was about glorifying Jesus Christ. However, it didn't stop when the last of those disciples died off. Jesus still lives today, and the Holy Spirit comes to abide in the lives of those who seek God intimately daily. Either our lives are conformed to this world or our lives are transformed by the Word of God. If your life is transformed by His Word, your walk today will look more like the walk of those disciples' years ago. I say the disciples instead of Jesus Christ because we are merely men and women in fleshly bodies who will battle choosing to live as the Bible teaches or living according to the desires of the flesh. However, our desires can change when we draw closer to Jesus just like the desires of those first disciple's lives changed. They were also merely men and women like us today, but drawing close to Jesus changed them from the inside - their heart.

Today, there are so many broken homes in America that multitudes of children are growing up with little stability, little love, no compassion for mankind, no roots, no dreams, nor any direction, etc. Many children today like myself, will grow up learning the basics of survival and eventually will face huge struggles within their own lives just as I did many years ago. The sad truth is that many never find anything worth living for and their lives end short. A life minus God is no life at all and until the Christian community realizes that this life is all about serving Jesus Christ instead of obtaining the American Dream, we will see hopelessness all over America because the multitudes fail to recognize and know God.

Praying to His Father one day, Jesus said, *"They have failed to see and recognize You Father!"*

John 16:1-3 (Weymouth New Testament) ¹These things I have spoken to you in order to clear stumbling-blocks out of your path. ²You will be excluded from the synagogues; nay more, the time is coming when anyone who has murdered one of you will suppose he is offering service to God. ³And they will do these things because they have failed to recognize the Father and to discover who I am.

Walking out into this cold and lonely world, it's hard enough just trying to exist, no wonder our perceptions are so cloudy that we are unable to see God in creation. We are unable to see just how glorious this world is, the natural wonders of this world in which God created such as:

- Mount Everest in Nepal
- Victoria Falls in Zambia/Zimbabwe
- Grand Canyon in Arizona, USA
- Great Barrier Reef in Australia
- Northern Lights
- Paricutin Volcano in Mexico
- Harbor of Rio de Janeiro, Brazil

The mountains in all their splendor and the rivers rushing to the seas, our earth holds so many sights which are so spectacular, yet we seldom think twice of just how these things came into existence. With all the pain so many of us endure in our lives, it is no wonder that we seldom even think about all the beautiful, glorious, and majestic creations in which God brought into existence. This world was planned out for us, His creation. Yes, in the beginning there was the Garden of Eden and it was supposed to be so wonderful.

However, just because we are not in that place, there are still glorious things all around us that let us know God is there! He is in that newborn baby. He is in that baby horse as it is being born. He is in the brilliant colorful flowers blooming in the spring. He is in the brilliant beauty of the stars and galaxies. He is in the smile of a loved one. He is in the compassion of those who step forth to help victims of floods and hurricanes which show kind-heartedness towards man-kind. He is in the miracles that happen every single day across the globe. He is in the healings, but He is also in the storms. If we never stop and pause, we will miss Him.

So, what does life minus God really look like? We must think about that question. Of course, the answer would depend on a few scenarios. In exploring this, I had to think back in my own life and what I determined were two different experiences of what life looks like minus God. First, life minus God looks totally different to those who have never known Him. Let me explain, in my own life growing up as a child and even into adolescence, my life was totally minus God. As I have said, I did not grow up in a home that knew God or Jesus Christ. There was much heartache and pain in my home. As I grew into the teen years, the pain was so intense that my life minus God seemed hopeless. When there is no God and there has never been any knowledge of Him, your storms are so fierce that you have no one to cry out to, no one to help carry you through the storms, and no valuable wisdom to turn to for understanding and guidance. Of course, there are many today who do not acknowledge there is a God and their life seems to be pretty good. However, every person will come to a place in their lives at some point where they can't save themselves, and the only One who can save them will be Jesus Christ.

When we do not acknowledge Jesus in our lives, things will seem hopeless many times, and we see suicide to be so prevalent among those whose lives are filled with hopelessness for whatever reason. I too several times contemplated committing suicide and even took measures to do so. I had no place to turn and no one to talk to other than maybe a few friends that also had no answers. I can remember the countless times I spent crying desperately in my room only wanting the pain to stop but never having the answers. I suppose that is why, so many turn to drugs, alcohol, or whatever seems to help numb the pain even though it is only temporary. Mine was drugs back in the 70s. The drugs helped me not be able to think about what my life looked like which was minus God. By the grace of God, I am only here today because He had other plans for my life which I could not see, and even though I did not know Him, He knew me! Overdosing several times, there was one incident where I died, left my body, and cried out to a God I didn't even know to give me another chance. One thing I still remember vividly about those days, God was always there and always trying to get my attention. Many people crossed my path in those days trying to pray for me and trying to share Jesus, but I was so wounded from pain that my walls which I built around me to keep others out were also not allowing Jesus to penetrate through. I did not want to hear about someone's God that I could not see. I wanted something tangible that could be seen to transform my life into purpose. Everyone desires purpose in this life; however, outside of God there is no purpose. God is good; He never stopped sending those across my path. The day finally came when I listened and listened and listened until I believed.

The second scenario of what life minus God looks like would be for those who have had an experience with Him but may have walked away from the church, from praying, or from seeking Him. Again, in my life there was a time that I gave up on the church, what we call the church today. When I did this, I also walked away from all those I had been connected to who were walking with Jesus. I even avoided everyone except those who were out in the world. I told myself that I hadn't walked away from God even though I really had. I told myself that I didn't need the advice or correction for that matter from those associates I had while in the church. In doing this, I surrounded myself with others who either did not know Jesus or those who had also chosen to walk back into the world. During this time, my storms were fiercer than they had ever been in my life. During this time, I knew the answers and the truth, but I chose not to follow that path. My life was minus God because I had chosen a pathway which was contrary to His way of living. In my fiercest storms, there were times because of guilt that I would not cry out to Him and then there were times that I would but only because I wanted Him to fix my life. In those times, I would wonder if He still loved me or if He still cared. Deep down inside, I always knew that He was still there, but He was waiting for that day I would choose Him all over again. Many times, the simple truth is that He has already forgiven us, but we have a hard time forgiving ourselves. I knew that my life could not get better unless my choices were to walk according to His ways not mine. So, in this scenario, life minus God was so painful because I knew truth and had compromised choosing a lie in hopes that God would intervene.

My fiercest storm was that of burying my oldest daughter who was killed at age 25 while I was not on the pathway God had chosen for me. This was the most painful time of my life and brought me to the place where I regretted that I had fallen away into a lifestyle which was not worthy of God. However, even though we make wrong choices, God is always there to accept us back with loving arms and cleanse us of all unrighteousness.

Life minus God is no life at all! Think about that. If God has given you life and He is void of everything you do, your life really has no purpose! Everyone desires to have purpose, we were created that way. God created mankind for purpose. If this were not so, we would merely exist just like animals. Yes, animals have purpose, but that purpose was created for man. God made animals for mankind. Animals and plants help to balance nature and preserve the environment through photosynthesis by plants and respiration by animals, making earth comfortable for human habitat. Other than that, animals were not created in the image of God and do not have the ability to do the things that man can do. Man can do so much more. We have the capability to think, reason, create, teach, learn, love, feel emotions, etc. However, these things mean absolutely nothing minus God in our lives! God created everything for good; however, everything we see today was NOT created by God. Most of the things we see especially within our cities were created by man using what God created. Let me emphasize this. When God created the heavens and the earth, all the animals and birds, the sea creatures, and man, He saw that it was good.

Genesis 1:31 (NLT) ³¹ Then God looked over all he had made, and he saw that it was very good! And evening passed and morning came, marking the sixth day.

All those things which God created are good, but I doubt that He looks down from heaven at the nightclubs and says, *"This is good!"* That is just one example, but I think you get my point. Man created so much of the things that we see, but they do not necessarily have God in them! Much of what we see today that man created has taken away from our relationship with God. God is all about relationship. He desires that we have a heartfelt relationship with Him. He desires that our relationships with our spouses, children, family, and friends are strong and intact. He desires that we develop relationships with strangers in order that they know Jesus. He desires that our heart be for others, the compassion of Jesus Christ. However, today much of our heart is turned towards inventions made by man instead of what is naturally created by God. With our hours spent on cell phones, computers, all the latest technology, our relationships suffer. Our children and loved ones are no longer nurtured in love and compassion. It is no wonder that we struggle in being able to love like God with all the distractions invented by man that surround our society.

Let me say that all the modern technology today was necessary for the Anti-Christ to one day rise and Jesus to come back, but at what cost is this to those who say they are Christians? Most Christians today are NOT really following in the same pathway as Jesus Christ. Most Christians today are NOT in love with God or the concept of following Him. Most Christians today are NOT willing to lay their lives down like in biblical days and follow Jesus Christ. Most Christians today know very little about the Holy Spirit which is the most important connection to knowing anything about God's Word. The Holy Spirit was sent to us in order that we come to know God's Word which is Truth and is the only thing that will set you free to live a life with God, not minus God. Most Christians today are really minus Jesus, minus God, minus being able to love, and minus the Truth.

How exactly can we walk like Jesus when we don't really know Him? How can we love Him when we don't really know Him? How can we even love our own families when we can't see what is Truth?

CHAPTER TWO
AS IN THE DAYS OF NOAH

Matthew 24:37-39 (ESV) [37] For as were the days of Noah, so will be the coming of the Son of Man. [38] For as in those days before the flood they were eating and drinking, marrying and giving in marriage, until the day when Noah entered the ark, [39] and they were unaware until the flood came and swept them all away, so will be the coming of the Son of Man.

We see these days manifested all around us. The day is fast approaching when Jesus will return for those who love Him and have been faithful to the gospels. Being faithful is following Truth. Jesus is Truth because He was in the beginning. He was the Word which is Truth and He was made flesh to live among us. *(John 1:1,14)* If we are not laying our lives down and picking up our own cross to follow Him, we are not living in Truth.

As in the days of Noah, there will be many eating and drinking, and carrying on in this world as everyone else does, totally unaware until that day. Many will be those who fall into the category of never knowing Him. They will find themselves in the fiercest storm just like all those in the days of Noah, and it will all be over with - too late to seek Him at that point.

There will also be many in those days that had known Him to some extent and for whatever reason had fallen away. As in the days of Noah, they will be busy with their focus on being conformed to this world just like the majority. This may be people who are actually in church weekly. A building will never save you. Just because people go to church does NOT make them Christians. Many may have never really known what it was like to have known Him intimately. An intimate relationship grows over time spent investing in that relationship.

Matthew 24:40-44 *40*Then two men will be in the field; one will be taken and one left. *41*Two women will be grinding at the mill; one will be taken and one left. *42*Therefore, stay awake, for you do not know on what day your Lord is coming. *43*But know this, that if the master of the house had known in what part of the night the thief was coming, he would have stayed awake and would not have let his house be broken into. *44*Therefore you also must be ready, for the Son of Man is coming at an hour you do not expect.

Your body is the house, the outer covering to your soul and your spirit. The thief is satan, and he has already come and broken into the homes of the majority, even those that claim to be Christians today. Your eyes and ears are the openings to your soul. Your soul is your will, your emotions, your personality, the very mechanism that controls your choices. Your spirit within is at war against your flesh which is the body, in order to bring light *(truth)* to your soul where your choices are to live as Christ. When we continually choose to allow our eyes to watch and read things which are contrary to the Word of God, we have allowed the enemy access into our home. When we continually choose to listen to the filth of this world, we have once again allowed the enemy access into our home. If the master of the house had known in what part of the night the thief was coming, he would have stayed awake and would not have let his house be broken into. When we make those choices to watch or listen to that which is NOT God, we have literally opened a door into our house. Your eyes and ears are the doors that allow either light or darkness to enter.

Jesus warns us in Matthew to stay awake! Staying awake means that we are to be awakened to the Truth. This is not referring to your natural state meaning to never sleep at night but your spiritual state which should be seeking, praying, and studying. If you are living your life according to His Word, your eyes will be awake to that which is false. If you are seeking God in order to find the narrow pathway, then your choices will be to guard your eyes and your ears so that they are both awake to know that which is NOT God! Either our spirit gains strength through time spent pouring the Word of God into our lives or our flesh gains strength and controls our soul where our choices are to be like everyone else in this world *(conformed)* which live as in the days of Noah.

What exactly does that mean? As in the days of Noah means that this world is doing exactly what they want to do because their desires are to be like this world, conformed to this world, like the people in this world. This is what your home *(your body, your life)* will look like when your choices are for the things in this world and not for the things of God. Either we store our treasures on earth or we store our treasures in heaven.

Matthew 24:45-51 45"Who then is the faithful and wise servant, whom his master has set over his household, to give them their food at the proper time? 46Blessed is that servant whom his master will find so doing when he comes. 47Truly, I say to you, he will set him over all his possessions. 48But if that wicked servant says to himself, 'My master is delayed,' ⁴⁹and begins to beat his fellow servants and eats and drinks with drunkards, ⁵⁰the master of that servant will come on a day when he does not expect him and at an hour he does not know ⁵¹and will cut him to pieces and put him with the hypocrites. In that place there will be weeping and gnashing of teeth.

We cannot live this life as if God is not real. We can't live this life looking for something tangible that we can touch and see. Our faith must rest in that which cannot be seen; otherwise, there is no hope! That which we cannot see created that which can be seen; therefore, would it not be true to say that the unseen is far greater than what can be seen? Jesus asks, *"Who then is faithful and wise?"* Being faithful is believing in what you cannot see. True wisdom only comes from the Father not from man. *(1 Corinthians 3:19-20)* The majority, as in the days of Noah, will be storing treasures on earth and trying to enjoy life in this world. If that is all you do, if this world is your primary focus, if this world has become your life, then you have no hope for eternity!

All things which man has invented were done so from what God created. Many of these things are necessary for God's plan to be completed, as I have stated. We all know that in the end, God wins! However, do we really know if we are on the right side of the fence? Are we really walking the narrow pathway? In my ministry, the pathways are discussed in depth. I have another book which will be published soon that will go into deep detail on the pathways because I feel that it is important to know if you are really on that narrow pathway or if you are traveling the wide pathway which leads to hell. However, according to Scripture, our walk with Jesus should look just like the walk of the disciple's years ago. Have we really walked away from the conformities of this world to follow Jesus? Are we trying to conform to this world by storing up treasures here on earth that we cannot take with us to Heaven, or are we storing up treasures in Heaven?

Our enemy, satan, is very real and he also has a plan. His plan is to make sure that the *"many"* are on the wide pathway which does NOT lead to Heaven. satan's plan is to make sure that the *"many"* love the things of this world so much that they do not have time to find the narrow pathway. Few even find the narrow pathway according to Scripture. *(Matthew 7:14)* This is something to think about because Jesus even warns us that there will be an alarming increase of false prophets in those days *(our days)* that are wolves in sheep clothing. It is amazing to me that most who claim to be Christians look so casually at these Scriptures. In fact, most who claim to be Christians believe they could recognize a false prophet or false teachings for that matter. The question is, just how much time do those who claim to be Christians really study the Word of God? The Bible tells us to study to show ourselves approved. I believe that most of us have forgotten how to really study. In high school or college, we had to really study in order to pass a test. Today, we try to just breeze by doing what we can by tithing perhaps and giving a little of our time to what we call the church. I have shared in my *"Boot Camp"* books how our walk should look like that of Paul. In fact, we normally begin our journey to find God by going to a church because we may be in the midst of a fierce storm in our lives and need God to fix it. Our journey begins with seeking God for what He can do for us. It begins with being all about what is in it for us. Going to church or seeking God to fix our lives is only the *"Way to Jesus."* We must have Truth in us to come to know God. If we never study, we will never mature. If we never mature, we will never find the Truth which sets us free.

John 8:31-33 (AMP) The Truth Will Make You Free
³¹ So Jesus was saying to the Jews who had believed Him, "If you abide in My word [continually obeying My teachings and living in accordance with them, <u>then] you are truly My disciples.</u> ³² And you will know the truth [regarding salvation], and the truth will set you free [from the penalty of sin]." ³³ They answered Him, "We are Abraham's descendants and have never been enslaved to anyone. What do You mean by saying, 'You will be set free'?"

Jesus said in order that we know Truth, in regard to salvation, we must first abide in His Word by obeying His teachings and living in accordance with His teachings. When we do this, only then are we His disciples. I'm not making this up, please reread the Scripture above. Jesus says that only those who abide in His Word and obey his teachings by living in accordance to those teachings are His disciples. Otherwise, you are merely living conformed to this world and you are NOT on that narrow pathway which leads to Heaven. The wide pathway does NOT lead to Heaven. When we live according to biblical teachings, we know the truth about salvation, but when we live as this world, we are in reality blinded to the Truth. I know when I stepped out from the mega-type churches because God sent me on a journey in the desert alone, my life radically changed. When we are separated from people where all we have is God, we find something far greater than we thought we knew when we were in the midst of the *"many"* who are all trying to follow Jesus according to man's methods which may be contrary to the Word of God. Far too often, what we think looks like God is not really God. Far too often, the teachings are not only contrary to the Word of God, but those leading the many are doing so for their own gain.

2 Peter 2:1-3 (ESV) False Prophets and Teachers [1]But false prophets also arose among the people, just as there will be false teachers among you, who will secretly bring in destructive heresies, even denying the Master who bought them, bringing upon themselves swift destruction. [2]And many will follow their sensuality, and because of them the way of truth will be blasphemed. [3]And in their greed they will exploit you with false words. Their condemnation from long ago is not idle, and their destruction is not asleep.

Let's continue reading more in John about how the Truth will set you free.

John 8:34-47 (AMP) [34] Jesus answered, "I assure you and most solemnly say to you, everyone who practices sin habitually is a slave of sin. [35] Now the slave does not remain in a household forever; the son [of the master] does remain forever. [36] So if the Son makes you free, then you are unquestionably free. [37] I know that you are Abraham's descendants; yet you plan to kill Me, because My word has no place [to grow] in you [and it makes no change in your heart].

The Word of God should change your heart. When we get so much of Jesus Christ on the inside of us, there will be a change. I remember when I began absorbing the Word of God daily, studying and studying, researching and researching, there was a distinct change within my life. However, it did not stop there. That change continued daily and still continues today. My choices changed and continue to do so because my desires changed. I found that I was not the same person at all who merely went to church, dedicated to the church, doing everything I could do to increase that building but not really listening to what God had planned specifically for my life and the calling He had placed on me. When my heart changed, I became broken for people. I became a disciple that wanted to live the rest of my life giving instead of taking, giving instead of receiving. Suddenly, I found that the things of this world were not as important as they once had been. I began to understand how the disciples in biblical days were able to walk away from the lives they once had to a life filled with Jesus.

Let's continue to look at those who believe themselves to be saved but in reality, they are living according to man's teachings not the teachings which Jesus brought.

John 8:38-47 (AMP) [38] I tell the things that I have seen at My Father's side [in His very presence]; so you also do the things that you heard from your father." [39] They answered, "Abraham is our father." Jesus said to them, "If you are [truly] Abraham's children, then do the works of Abraham and follow his example. [40] But as it is, you want to kill Me, a Man who has told you the truth, which I heard from God. This is not the way Abraham acted. [41] You are doing the works of your [own] father." They said to Him, "We are not illegitimate children; we have one [spiritual] Father: God." [42] Jesus said to them, "If

God were your Father [but He is not], you would love and recognize Me, for I came from God [out of His very presence] and have arrived here. For I have not even come on My own initiative [as self-appointed], but He [is the One who] sent Me. ⁴³ Why do you misunderstand what I am saying? It is because [your spiritual ears are deaf and] you are unable to hear [the truth of] My word. ⁴⁴ You are of your father the devil, and it is your will to practice the desires [which are characteristic] of your father. He was a murderer from the beginning, and does not stand in the truth because there is no truth in him. When he lies, he speaks what is natural to him, for he is a liar and the father of lies and half-truths. ⁴⁵ But because I speak the truth, you do not believe Me [and continue in your unbelief]. ⁴⁶ Which one of you [has proof and] convicts Me of sin? If I speak truth, why do you not believe Me? ⁴⁷ Whoever is of God and belongs to Him hears [the truth of] God's words; for this reason you do not hear them: because you are not of God and you are not in fellowship with Him."

There is no straddling the fence and there is no gray area. We either choose to live a life conformed to this world which is NOT God, or we choose to live a life which is set free from this world. In being set free, we choose Truth. Jesus Christ is Truth. To choose Truth, we must study the Word of God which is Truth. When we study, we will grow in Truth and our desires will change.

What are we set free from? Well for one, we are set free from the bondage of this world. The Truth, God's Word, opens our eyes that we can see what God is trying to reveal to us. The Truth, opens our ears where we can hear and discern if that message being taught really lines up with the Word of God. When we begin to see real Truth, we will either make a choice to remain living in our sinful state, or we will walk away from the desires of this world and choose to walk as Paul walked. We will choose to seek in order to find that narrow pathway just like Paul. We will begin running this race instead of just walking because we will realize there is so much more to Christianity and it is not about just finding the Way; it is not about just finding the Truth; it becomes about finding the Life!

John 14:6 (NKJV) Jesus said to him, "I am the way, the truth, and the life. No one comes to the Father except through Me.

Our heart will become one that says, *"Lord, I don't care if there is anything in this walk for me, and it's not even about what I can do for You Lord. It's all about living in Your Presence Lord, every day!"*

As we fast approach the coming of our Lord Jesus Christ, there will be many choices to make if we desire to stand before God one day as He tells us to enter the gates of Heaven. If your choices today are not to seek Him to a greater degree in order that you find that pathway, this life here on earth is the only life you will ever experience. This life on earth is NOT the life in which Jesus taught about. I pray as you read this book that your desires rise to seek God to a greater degree until you find Him.

Remember, God desires that none should perish! God is never in a hurry and He is never late. He continues to be patient to give all of us the opportunity to make the necessary changes in our lives where we include Him. This will include seeking Him to that degree where you find Him. I am amazed at how many people I meet that say they believe in God but have never heard His voice. I believe many times they do hear His voice, but they do not recognize that it is the voice of God or the Holy Spirit for that matter. We are always listening to voices, whether it be our own voice, the Holy Spirit, or our enemy. The distinction is that your voice will lead you to a life of selfishness which is totally okay with our enemy. If your desires are all about you, the enemy does not have to do very much because your own desires will lead to your destruction. However, there are two other voices. One is the enemy and his voice will be totally contrary to what the Word of God says while the Holy Spirit's voice will line up with the Word of God. The sad part is that a lot of what comes from our pulpits today does not line up with the Word of God. The sad part is that most people do not even realize it doesn't line up with the Word because they have never really studied to know the Word. In fact, most people do not even realize that the Word of God says in 3 places that there is NO need that man should teach you because in those days *(which are our days)* God will burn His Words in our hearts. You will find this first in the Old Testament.

Jeremiah 31:33-34 (NKJV) ³³But this is the covenant that I will make with the house of Israel after those days, says the Lord: I will put My law in their minds, and write it on their hearts; and I will be their God, and they shall be My people. ³⁴<u>No more shall every man teach his neighbor, and every man his brother, saying, 'Know the Lord,' for they all shall know Me, from the least of them to the greatest of them, says the Lord</u>. For I will forgive their iniquity, and their sin I will remember no more."

You can also read the same Scripture in the New Testament which was taught for all those who chose to follow Jesus, Jews and Gentiles. It is noted in Hebrews 8:10-11 which is the same as in Jeremiah and then in 1 John below, it is worded differently and was preached to all people.

1 John 2:26-27 (NKJV) [26]These things I have written to you concerning those who try to deceive you. [27]But the anointing which you have received from Him abides in you, and <u>you do not need that anyone teach you;</u> but as the same anointing teaches you concerning all things, **and is true, and is not a lie,** and just as it has taught you, you will abide in Him.

If you read all of 1 John 2, John first began sharing with those who were following Jesus, a basic test for them to be able to see if they really KNEW Him, Jesus Christ. Then John talks about their spiritual state. John continues teaching on the importance of not loving this world because if we do love this world, the love of the Father is NOT in us. He continues teaching them about the deceptions which will be faced in those last hours which is referring to all the false prophets, teachings, etc. John continues from here to share how the truth abides in us **IF** what we heard from the beginning also abides in us. Teachings from the beginning would be the full teachings which Jesus taught while He walked with the disciples. This would mean for us today that we must be following the TRUE teachings from the Word of God. Was it not emphasized above that the anointing, which comes from the Holy Spirit, would teach us ALL THINGS which are TRUE and not a LIE. I believe there were concerns about deception in those days as well maybe because there were some who claimed to be followers of Jesus that would follow teachings of man and NOT the anointed teachings of the Holy Spirit. John continues from that point to teach about the deceptions that will come upon this world as we know it because of false teachings. John tells us that we have the anointing; do you have the anointing today? You should be filled with the anointing daily. The anointing from God only comes if His presence is living within you. Jesus told His disciples that it was better that He left in order that the Holy Spirit would come. *(John 16:7)* The Holy Spirit is the presence of God that should be dwelling inside of us and if it is, we have that anointing. If you do have the anointing, then John says that the anointing you have, should be the One teaching you - not man, so that you are NOT deceived! Did Jesus not tell us that the Holy Spirit would be the One who teaches us?

John 16:13-15 (ESV) ¹³The Holy Spirit is coming. He will lead you into all truth. He will not speak His Own words. He will speak what He hears. He will tell you of things to come. ¹⁴He will honor Me. He will receive what is Mine and will tell it to you. ¹⁵Everything the Father has is Mine. That is why I said to you, 'He will receive what is Mine and will tell it to you.'

You see, the Holy Spirit's job has always been to be our teacher. He cannot teach us when we run to man to do so. I'm not saying that we are not to be joined together with other believers, but I will say that most churches today do not look like the church in Acts. Much of what is being taught today is taught out of context. You cannot pick and choose pieces of Scripture to determine what God was trying to show us. When I teach, I do choose certain sections of Scripture many times instead of reading the whole chapter to those I am ministering to because of either the timeframe or because I choose to just read the part that I am emphasizing. Prior to teaching that part of Scripture, I have already studied the whole section to gain the revelation needed where my teaching is accurate. However, I am quick to point out that I am NOT God; I am NOT Jesus, and I am perfectly capable of being wrong. You don't find many preachers today that will admit they can be wrong. Maybe they know this, but they never say it. Not all preachers agree on what is being taught among the different ministries today or the different denominations, yet they believe they are the ones correct. However, someone must be wrong. I'm okay with admitting this because I know as I continue to grow, God shows me things that I may not have seen a year ago. My point is that as I teach others, my job is only to stir up that desire in them so that they go back to the Word of God to seek Him for themselves. Over the years, I have stirred up people who have come to me saying they disagreed with what I taught, but they went on to tell me that this had stirred them up to go back to Scripture to prove me wrong! Glory to God! When I stir people up to make them go seek God to a greater degree, I have done what God has called me to do, and I hope that those who read this book will also do the same!

Making it to heaven is not about being right on everything you study in the Word of God, it is totally about having that intimate relationship with God the Father, God the Son, and God the Holy Spirit. God has never called us to be perfect only humble and obedient by sharing Jesus Christ to this world. However, the church as we know it today in America has failed miserably because their motivation has become to be *"aquarium keepers"* instead of training those who come and turning them loose out into the world to share the gospel. For some reason, pastors believe that those who sit up under their teachings belong to them. I have literally seen leaders of huge churches fight over people as they claim they were their fruit to begin with and in their group and another leader stole them. Are you kidding me? The only fruit I know of is the fruit of the spirit and the things I have witnessed far too many times in the churches has sickened me because none of us own any of the people. If they are followers of Jesus Christ, they belong to Him. If they are followers of Jesus Christ, they do not belong to a particular ministry or a certain pastor or priest, they belong to Jesus Christ. I have come to the place in my life when asked what denomination I am, my response is, *"I am of NO denomination; I am a disciple of Jesus Christ!"* As a disciple of Jesus Christ, our aim must be to take the gospel to the world in Truth, and our motivation must never be for gain in any way.

As in the days of Noah, I'm sure there were those who thought they knew God but only knew of Him. As in those days, we can also see that only few were on the right path which led to life, Noah and his family. Today, we have so much more than in those days to help us on this journey. As John taught, we have that anointing or at least we can have that anointing. If we are chasing after the anointing instead of running towards a man-made ministry, will we not have a better chance of being one of those *"few"* who find the Truth which will set us free from this world?

CHAPTER THREE
FOR THE LEAST OF THESE

In Chapter Two, we read Matthew 24 beginning with verse 37 *(As in the days of Noah...)*; however, we need to look at what Jesus was teaching prior to verse 37 and going forward into Matthew 25. Prior to verse 37, Jesus was teaching about the signs of the end of this age. Following the signs, he began teaching about the Tribulation Period as told by the prophet Daniel. After the Tribulation teaching, Jesus shared about the coming of the Son of Man and then we come to verse 37 which was discussed in detail. However, we need to understand verse 37 was where Jesus began warning those who would choose to listen, that they must study in order to know the signs. We need to be able to envision the tribulation period so that we understand what is coming and can believe that Jesus will be returning. All these things He mentions must take place prior to His coming back. However, Jesus continued to teach that He would be coming back in a day and time like that of the days of Noah. In other words, the people's hearts would be the same as in those days. Their hearts would not be for God but for this world. Their choices would be for this world. For the few that would listen and adhere to His teachings, these words were to help them to see truth with their eyes and ears. These teachings were for those who would listen in order that they would be able to recognize that which was false.

Immediately following Chapter 24 and going into Chapter 25, Jesus began sharing parables. These parables flow together. The first parable was of *The Ten Virgins* which is all about being prepared once again. The parable following *The Ten Virgins* is called *The Talents* which is all about how we are preparing and spending our time while waiting for His return. Following this parable, He speaks of *The Final Judgment* which is where I will begin.

Matthew 25:31-46 (ESV) The Final Judgment
31"When the Son of Man comes in his glory, and all the angels with him, then he will sit on his glorious throne. 32Before him will be gathered all the nations, and he will separate people one from another as a shepherd separates the sheep from the goats. 33And he will place the sheep on his right, but the goats on the left. 34 Then the King will say to those on his right, 'Come, you who are blessed by my Father, inherit the kingdom prepared for you from the foundation of the world. 35 For I was hungry and you gave me food, I was thirsty and you gave me drink, I was a stranger and you welcomed me, 36 I was naked and you clothed me, I was sick and you visited me, I was in prison and you came to me.' 37 Then the righteous will answer him, saying, 'Lord, when did we see you hungry and feed you, or thirsty and give you drink? 38 And when did we see you a stranger and welcome you, or naked and clothe you? 39 And when did we see you sick or in prison and visit you?' 40 And the King will answer them, 'Truly, I say to you, as you did it to one of the least of these my brothers, you did it to me.'

We need to really look at this to see if our lives really portray a life which is following Jesus. This is where the sheep are separated from the goats. There are core elements here that distinguish the sheep from the goats. The sheep were those who gave of their lives for other people. This is not something we do lightly. This is something that we do from the heart. What is in your heart will determine what category you fit in. Just as this book says, *"I can't make you love Him,"* I also cannot make you have a heart for people. We can drop money in the offering plate all day long at our local churches and claim that some of that money goes to help feed and clothe the least of these, but this is not what we see here. Having a heart for people is being engaged on the battlefield. It is not about taking a few seconds to give someone else the money and not have any involvement yourself. I tell those I minister to all the time that Jesus had one purpose; Jesus had one focus; Jesus died for one reason and that was for people. If we are to be like Jesus, we will have a heart for people. Our focus and our calling on this earth will be for people. In whatever capacity that God calls you, it will involve people. It is about feeding them naturally and spiritually. Jesus continues as He addresses the goats.

[41] "Then he will say to those on his left, 'Depart from me, you cursed, into the eternal fire prepared for the devil and his angels. [42] For I was hungry and you gave me no food, I was thirsty and you gave me no drink, [43] I was a stranger and you did not welcome me, naked and you did not clothe me, sick and in prison and you did not visit me.' [44] Then they also will answer, saying, 'Lord, when did we see you hungry or thirsty or a stranger or naked or sick or in prison, and did not minister to you?' [45] Then he will answer them, saying, 'Truly, I say to you, as you did not do it to one of the least of these, you did not do it to me.' [46] And these will go away into eternal punishment, but the righteous into eternal life."

In the final judgment, we see that the sheep are separated from the goats. The distinction between the two, the sheep were all about spending their time feeding, ministering, clothing, and being a friend to those who were the least of these and the goats did not. The goats chose to do none of these things.

Let me share a message that I gave sometime back on the streets. If you are a sheep, you are all about investing in relationships and especially into the one relationship that really matters, Jesus Christ. However, without really knowing God, you will never be able to love. I am not talking about the world kind of love but the God-kind of love. Without really knowing Him, you will never be a sheep. Our churches today are full of goats which have been trained to act like sheep, but they are not sheep. A sheep will be one who does what Jesus said. They will be separated in that day from the goats. If you are a sheep, it is in your heart. You can spend the rest of your life pretending to be a sheep, but the truth will all come out the day you stand before God because He looks at your heart.

In my message about the sheep and goats, there are several things I teach. First, we must understand that satan IS NOT stupid! He comes as a wolf in sheep clothing, and Jesus tells us that *"many"* will be led astray.

Matthew 24:4-5 (ESV) ⁴And Jesus answered them, "See that no one leads you astray. ⁵For many will come in my name saying, 'I am the Christ,' and they will lead many astray.

Jesus also tells us that those who are His sheep hear His voice and follow that voice.

John 10:27 (NKJV) My sheep hear My voice, and I know them, and they follow Me.

If you study sheep and goats in the natural, you will find that sheep follow ONE master, one voice. On the other hand, goats are never satisfied and are always looking to see if the grass is greener on the other side. Goats always want more and are never satisfied with less. Goats want to be the ONE in charge. In many churches today, the goats always desire to be the leaders and in large ministries, there are many which are put in charge of the people to keep the flock intact. I have been in this very scenario. In the large churches, those in charge are always right and those not in charge are to follow the voice of the ones in charge! However, sheep only follow ONE voice and that voice IS NOT a pastor or leader within a church. Jesus should be over every church today but that is NOT the case. If He is the head of the church, a pastor or priest will not be the one being increased and acknowledge. Let me emphasize this a minute, my daughter attends a church where their pastor does not like to be addressed as *"pastor"* because he is merely a man. He prefers that the adults call him by his first name. However, out of respect, the children do address him as pastor. This same pastor chooses not to be paid for what God has called him to do. I was amazed because in America, most pastors desire to be known and increased. In fact, people normally refer to certain mega-type churches as *"Pastor so and so's church."* When did it stop being Jesus' church? It stopped being Jesus' church when man determined that they could gain material wealth and fame by using their own methods instead of the teachings which

Jesus gave. We are to follow one voice as I stated and that will NOT be the voice of a man.

When we are talking about following a voice, it is with our ears that we hear and listen and make the choice what voice we are going to follow. Our eyes are to be trained to look away from that which is NOT truth because the enemy will try to entice us through what we see in order that we stumble. Our eyes and ears are the very openings to our heart, and it is imperative that we listen to the ONE voice that will NOT lead us down the path which leads to hell! It is imperative that we find that narrow path because Jesus tells us that few will find it! It is important that we are grounded in Scripture in order that we do not fall into the category of the *"many"* which will be led astray! It is important that we know the Holy Spirit was sent to us, in order, to teach us so that in those days (the days of Noah), we understand it is okay to be joined together with other believers, but we know the voice we should be following which is that of the Holy Spirit and NOT of man!

The enemy daily causes stumbling blocks in order that the majority follow the wrong pathway. One of the main stumbling blocks to those that call themselves Christians is striving to live a life conformed to this world. This can be done in such ways as being joined together with other believers based on attending the largest churches which have all the comforts of this world. We want the best! We want a church that is vibrant! We want the coffee shops, the children's programs, and the social aspect of walking this walk out with the large crowds! I have been there, and it is great to have many Christian friends fellowshipping together under one roof weekly, attending the same retreats, conferences, or social events. However, Jesus said the *"many"* will NOT even find the narrow pathway. The truth is that we feel more secure when we know we are following a larger crowd than following a few whose messages are a bit harsh and to the point. We want to believe that Jesus didn't REALLY mean for us to give up things in this world which are really not harmful. We want to believe that if we attend a good church, give our tithes, and follow what that man or woman on the pulpit says, everything is great, and we must be on that narrow pathway. However, this is the way goats think and the way they have been trained to believe.

It is imperative that we find that narrow pathway, and I promise you it is NOT going to look like the pathway most Christians are on. However, once you find it, you will know you are on the right path. Once you find it, your focus must be on hearing the voice of the Holy Spirit. God does desire that none should perish, but it will be your choice as to which pathway you choose.

Your eyes will remain focused on the journey if you are following the ONE true Master. On this journey, if you are truly following the voice of the Holy Spirit, you will stay on that pathway through your trials, tests, storms, and persecution. What we seldom see among those that claim to be Christians today is the persecution, especially in America; however, Jesus tells us that if they hated Him they will also hate us. If they persecuted Him, they will persecute us. If you are following the true voice of the Holy Spirit, you will be hated and persecuted. Most of the time, your persecution will be from those who call themselves Christians, not unbelievers. In my life, I have been persecuted by what we call the church for being too radical, for teaching Revelation, for teaching about the Holy Spirit, and even for stepping out to attend Bible studies which were NOT from members of the church I was connected to. I was even asked to either leave or to stop doing those things we are called to do by Jesus. The outcome was that I walked away because ultimately, I choose to follow the voice of the One true God! So, I know too well what persecution looks like. The good news is that when you experience this, you know you may very well be on that narrow pathway because there will be few there with you. Once you experience this, your walk begins to be one that is closer to Jesus Christ than ever before because you do not have all your little Christian circles anymore to run to for whatever trial you are going through. What you do have is a Savoir that continues to pour into you more truth so that you are set free from this world. At this place, your experiences become the avenues of growth into the spiritual realm that you may never have experienced before. You experience your battles as He leads you through knowing that the outcome will be His outcome! Your worries subside because you know that He oversees your life and you take one day at a time totally surrendered to Him. Your faith says, *"Lord, You have the outcome and even if I don't understand, I know the end result will be Your plan."* Most Christians today do not experience this kind of relationship with God. Most Christians today are satisfied with attending their church of preference and living a good life with the *"majority"* that call themselves Christians.

We know that Jesus teaches of the days of Noah, and we know the day will come when the sheep and goats are separated. We also know that the *"majority"* that call themselves Christians are really goats who have been trained to act like sheep because there are multitudes in our churches today and the Scriptures say that the *"many"* will stand before God and be sent to hell. This prophecy cannot be changed; however, there are many today that are sheep which are caught in the middle by being engaged under a ministry which is teaching false. The hope is that those who have chosen to step out and teach truth touch the lives of those who are listening that they will seek Jesus to a deeper level.

In biblical days they had *"Gatekeepers!"* Gatekeepers were watchmen who were there to protect the Lord's House. They were there to defend the gospels and the truth of the gospels. This is not being done today in most of the churches which call themselves the House of God. Gatekeepers, just like in biblical days, will be those who are bold enough to speak out against the sins of the church. Gatekeepers will be mocked, hated, and kicked out of the modern-day churches. Gatekeepers have a huge responsibility to keep people on the right path where they do NOT drift away from the Lord. They are not afraid to tell the truth of God's Word even though their messages will not be popular to the *"majority."* Their motivation will be to save as many as they can from the fires of eternal hell. In biblical days and like today, gatekeepers will be those who keep watch for the Master's return. They will watch for the signs of the times which most churches do not do. Their messages will be like those of John the Baptist, bold and harsh as they prepare people for the second coming of Jesus Christ. Shame on those pastors that want to try and teach their followers how to live a good Christian life here on this earth because preparing for the second coming of Jesus Christ has nothing to do with being blessed with the riches and conformities of this world. Jesus tells us that we will suffer on this earth. He tells us that we will be hated and persecuted. Yet, we want to say that God has blessed us because our life here on this earth has been very fortunate where we have made a good living, acquired money in the bank, prosperity, etc. If you proclaim Jesus Christ in all truth, you are going to be persecuted. We are seeing the *"few"* Christians today that have been singled out for their belief and all hell has broken loose on their lives. Some of these headlines have been broadcast all over America which has astounded the Christian community. Those suffering and being persecuted because they refuse to make wedding cakes for same sex marriages or issue marriage license to the same, this is the persecution that Jesus said was coming. However, how many are really willing to stand firm on biblical beliefs when they are singled out and may lose everything they have worked hard for? These days are here and there will be more persecutions. We should count it all joy when we are the target of the hate and animosity of this world knowing that maybe we have done something right. Just maybe we are entering that narrow pathway and we should rejoice even if we lose everything. Christianity today and being a gatekeeper means that we are willing to suffer for Jesus Christ by being bold and going where most people who call themselves Christians will never go. It means stepping out and proclaiming what the majority will never proclaim. We must understand that when we are willing to step out and speak those bold messages, the majority will not follow us. We must understand that having a church building was never meant to gain numbers and hold onto that flock as if it belongs to us. Jesus said to *"go"* to all who claim to be His followers and to those who do not know Him to spread the gospel. He never said to stay! We get comfortable in our church buildings and we miss our ministry that He is calling us to. The majority did not follow Jesus Christ, only the few. The majority came to listen, but the majority walked away. The reason they will not stay when the messages are spoken in boldness and truth is because goats DO NOT want to follow the narrow pathway. That pathway requires too much, and it is not an easy road to travel. They did not follow Jesus and they will NOT follow you if you are proclaiming the Truth! Why would we think that we can build a ministry of thousands when Jesus did not build such a ministry? They came to see what He was about; they came for healing; they came for food, but the majority walked away and only the few remained.

If you will study John 6, you will see where Jesus fed the five thousand. The Bible says they followed Him because they saw His signs of healing. This would be those who attend church to see what is in it for them! Here was where they witnessed Jesus multiplying the food in order to feed them. Today, if we were to witness such a miracle, would we follow that miracle or go back home? We would probably follow the miracle as long as there was something in it for us but when that ended, we would go back home. Further down in John 6, the following day, many of the people were looking for Him and Jesus tells them that they were not seeking Him because of the signs but because they had eaten of the loaves and were filled. Jesus goes on to say, *"Do not labor for the food which perishes but for the food which endures everlasting life."* This pretty much shows us that the people wanted to be fed once again. It was not about the words which He spoke which gives life, it was about what they could gain for themselves. If you continue reading John 6, you will see where the people began murmuring and complaining because they desired that Jesus poured out of heaven manna, the bread as their ancestors received daily in order that they would be fed. Jesus tells them that He is the bread of life and those who come to Him would never hunger; however, the people did not believe in Him. They only wanted to follow the signs which could be seen in the natural not the spiritual signs; they only wanted to be fed. In verse 45, Jesus tells them that those who come to Him would be those that are taught by God, those who have heard and learned from the Father. Once again there is confirmation that we are to be taught by God which is the Holy Spirit. The Holy Spirit is the presence of God within us. Finally, the people walked away, and Jesus said to His disciples, the twelve, *"Do you also want to go away?"*

I was given a vision one day. In that vision, I saw a great crowd of people as I looked at what we call the church. Multitudes were not going the right way. Great crowds of people everywhere and no one facing the same way as another. Everyone was going about their lives and looking in different directions, scattering themselves about. None concerned with where they were headed and walking in whatever direction without any consideration. As I looked and gazed at what we call the church today, I was troubled by what I saw, for so many were blinded as they strived so hard to be conformed to this world.

Yes, the majority of the churches we see today are as in the days of Noah! If our true desire is to be a sheep, we must lay hold to the teachings of Jesus Christ.

Matthew 6:19-24 (AMP) [19] "Do not store up for yourselves [material] treasures on earth, where moth and rust destroy, and where thieves break in and steal. [20] But store up for yourselves treasures in heaven, where neither moth nor rust destroys, and where thieves do not break in and steal; [21] for where your treasure is, there your heart [your wishes, your desires; that on which your life centers] will be also. [22] "The eye is the lamp of the body; so if your eye is clear [spiritually perceptive], your whole body will be full of light [benefiting from God's precepts]. [23] But if your eye is bad [spiritually blind], your whole body will be full of darkness [devoid of God's precepts]. <u>So if the [very] light inside you [your inner self, your heart, your conscience] is darkness, how great and terrible is that darkness!</u> [24] "No one can serve two masters; for either he will hate the one and love the other, or he will be devoted to the one and despise the other. You cannot serve God and mammon [money, possessions, fame, status, or whatever is valued more than the Lord].

Let me emphasize what we consider is in our heart. Notice, that Jesus said, *"If the light inside of you is really darkness."* Most people who believe they are following truth believe that they have light in their heart. This is really the scary part because suppose what you think is light is really darkness. It is much harder to save someone who believes they are already good with God than someone who knows that there is darkness in their heart or even areas that need to be improved. Jesus is trying to show us that those who believe what is in their heart is light but is really darkness, the darkness in their heart is much darker than those who know they are not right with God. This goes back to Revelation, it is much better to be cold than lukewarm with God where He makes it clear that He will spit you out of His mouth. *(Revelation 3:15)* I have heard so many people who claim to be Christians boastfully state that their walk with God was all good, yet, there were many things I witnessed that was NOT living a godly life. Beware, that you think more highly of yourself than you should. Daily, our lives should be focused on seeking Him deeper so that our heart changes on the inside which ultimately portrays a holy-lifestyle on the outside. Only then will we live out our lives as a sheep and not a goat. Whoa to those who think that they are something that they are not. It is better to be cold than lukewarm, but we must strive to be on fire for God.

Through this journey with God, whatever is in your heart proceeds out of your mouth. What we choose to watch, read, and listen will determine what is on the inside of us. Nothing on the inside of you, your thoughts, desires, or motivations were born inside of you when you came out of your mother's womb. What is inside of you depends on what you have spent your time doing. What you read, what you watch on television or the computer, and the company you keep have programed your way of thinking. The good news is that all those things can be reprogrammed if your desire is to have that heartfelt relationship with Jesus Christ. You can be one of His sheep following the pathway He has chosen for you, but only if your desires change. The outcome of your life will be determined based on your eyes and ears as you make daily choices to the doors you open.

Matthew 15:13-19 (ESV) ⁱ³ He answered, "Every plant that my heavenly Father has not planted will be rooted up. ¹⁴ Let them alone; they are blind guides. And if the blind lead the blind, both will fall into a pit." ¹⁵ But Peter said to him, "Explain the parable to us." ¹⁶ And he said, "Are you also still without understanding? ¹⁷ Do you not see that whatever goes into the mouth passes into the stomach and is expelled? ¹⁸ But what comes out of the mouth proceeds from the heart, and this defiles a person. ¹⁹ For out of the heart come evil thoughts, murder, adultery, sexual immorality, theft, <u>false witness</u>, slander.

Our enemy, satan, has been very successful at making sure the *"Christians"* are NOT fed Truth! As I have stated, false witnesses are all around us today. If satan cannot keep you out of church, you can bet that he will defile the church in order that the majority go down with him. Remember, if you are not seeking God intimately yourself and all your knowledge of the Word of God has come from man's teachings, you are probably deceived. If you are following the crowds and not questioning everything around you, you are probably NOT on that narrow pathway! Your ministry individually should look like John the Baptist or the disciples of yesterday. Our motivation in this world should be for people just like it was during biblical days for those who were really sheep. Our lives should live and breathe Scripture so that we go forth to share bold messages of truth to those who are lowly. If you are the lowly of this world, know that Jesus Christ came for you, but once He gets a hold of your life, He will also raise you up to be one of His disciples with a mission for others who were once where you were!

1 Corinthians 1:21-31 English Standard Version (ESV) 21 For since, in the wisdom of God, the world did not know God through wisdom, it pleased God through the folly of what we preach to save those who believe. 22 For Jews demand signs and Greeks seek wisdom, 23 but we preach Christ crucified, a stumbling block to Jews and folly to Gentiles, 24 but to those who are called, both Jews and Greeks, Christ the power of God and the wisdom of God. 25 For the foolishness of God is wiser than men, and the weakness of God is stronger than men. 26 For consider your calling, brothers: not many of you were wise according to worldly standards, not many were powerful, not many were of noble birth. 27 But God chose what is foolish in the world to shame the wise; God chose what is weak in the world to shame the strong; 28 God chose what is low and despised in the world, even things that are not, to bring to nothing things that are, 29 so that no human being might boast in the presence of God. 30 And because of him you are in Christ Jesus, who became to us wisdom from God, righteousness and sanctification and redemption, 31 so that, as it is written, "Let the one who boasts, boast in the Lord."

Jesus came for those who are lowly. He came for those who are considered the *"nobody's"* in this world. It's not that He is not here for everyone, but Jesus clearly said that He came NOT for those who do not need a physician.

Matthew 9:10-13 (ESV) 10 And as Jesus reclined at table in the house, behold, many tax collectors and sinners came and were reclining with Jesus and his disciples. 11 And when the Pharisees saw this, they said to his disciples, "Why does your teacher eat with tax collectors and sinners?" 12 But when he heard it, he said, "Those who are well have no need of a physician, but those who are sick. ¹³ Go and learn what this means: 'I desire mercy, and not sacrifice.' For I came not to call the righteous, but sinners."

So, here we are. We may know that we are considered the lowly but in this low place many times we feel angry. Perhaps we feel dissatisfied. Perhaps we question, "God, why am I in this place in my life?" When I first began my ministry to the homeless, I remember that I thought I was going to share the Truth with them, set them free so they would get off the streets, get a job, home, etc. However, the first thing God showed me was that my thinking was wrong. Who am I to say if they are to remain on the streets or live in a house? How do we know what God desires for them? You see, our way of thinking is NOT the way God thinks as He clearly tells us.

Isaiah 55:8-9 (ESV) ⁸For my thoughts are not your thoughts, neither are your ways my ways, declares the Lord. ⁹ For as the heavens are higher than the earth, so are my ways higher than your ways and my thoughts than your thoughts.

God also tells us that wisdom of this world is foolishness.

1 Corinthians 3:18-23 (ESV) ¹⁸Let no one deceive himself. If anyone among you thinks that he is wise in this age, let him become a fool that he may become wise. ¹⁹ For the wisdom of this world is folly with God. For it is written, "He catches the wise in their craftiness," ²⁰ and again, "The Lord knows the thoughts of the wise, that they are futile." ²¹ So let no one boast in men. For all things are yours, ²² *whether Paul or Apollos or Cephas or the world or life or death or the present or the future—all are yours,* ²³ *and you are Christ's, and Christ is God's.*

My job on the streets was to just share Jesus. It was to just share and give them hope. The hope does not have to come in the form of a job, house, etc. Our hope comes in knowing that He loves us! Our hope comes in knowing that He died for us! Our hope comes in knowing that He desires to walk with us, lead and guide us through the still waters and through the storms. He desires to teach us all things which are TRUTH! Jesus desires to live with you today, tomorrow, and forever. Our only part is running to Him not from Him.

Being on the streets ministering to the lowly taught me so much and continues to do so. I see those on the streets knowing so much more about the Word of God than I do those sitting on a pew week after week in church listening to a pastor and never reading the Word of God. Many of those on the streets are continually studying the Word of God because their focus in this life is NOT about keeping up with the Jones' in all the capacity of storing your treasure on earth instead of in Heaven. This life is temporal and is passing away as we know it. Most in this world will have a hard time letting go of all their possessions to live a holy life with the Holy Spirit by their side.

Who are the lowly of this world? Have you ever really thought about that? God chooses those in lowly places because He does not need the man or woman who is educated of this world to lead His people. He doesn't need the man or woman who has become successful in this world to show others how to also be successful in this world. This day and age of technology has destroyed relationships in this world compared to days without. God chooses those that no one else would have chosen. God chose Moses even though he had a stutter and felt incapable of doing what God was calling him to do. God chose me to be a speaker even though I was the only student in my class during high school that would take an *"F"* on a paper if it had to be read orally in front of the class. I had no self-esteem; I felt that I wasn't good enough because of my upbringing. In my home as a child, my mother was an alcoholic. I was raised being told that I would never amount to anything. I was told that I was not pretty enough, smart enough, etc. As a child, you grow up believing what you are told. However, God looked down on me and said, *"I will choose her to rise up and be a minister one day. She will stand to teach and preach to all those I send across her pathway."* Yes, God has a sense of humor. He groomed me for this prior to it ever happening. I was placed in a job where I became their public speaker. I either spoke to the crowds or I didn't get paid. The first time I stood in front of a group of people, it was horrible; however, I changed the way I spoke because I knew that in order for me to share with others, it had to be something I believed in. In other words, it had to come from the heart. I wound up speaking to groups of 100s at one point and was recognized as a gifted speaker. However, all of this was God preparing me for where He was sending me. I was one of the lowly. I was a no-body and today, I am only who I am because of Him. I can only do what I do because of Him. You can be whatever God has called you to be because you will do it through Him. If He chooses you, He will see you through!

CHAPTER FOUR
LOVING FROM THE INSIDE

Loving from the inside is merely loving from the heart. Your heart cannot and never will love like God loves if it is not filled with God. God is love; He is the definition of love. It is not love as the world loves which most of the time is all about what is in it for *"me."* Yes, it does matter what we choose to watch and what we choose to listen to. As in previous chapters, we should always guard our eyes and ears so that we walk in truth at all times and are not deceived by that which is false. Our eyes and our ears are the only openings which lead to our heart. If you desire that your love be pure, and your heart be pure, you must guard your eyes and ears.

Psalm 51:9-17 (NIV) [9]Hide your face from my sins and blot out all my iniquity. [10]Create in me a pure heart, O God, and renew a steadfast spirit within me. [11]Do not cast me from your presence or take your Holy Spirit from me. [12]Restore to me the joy of your salvation and grant me a willing spirit, to sustain me. [13]Then I will teach transgressors your ways, so that sinners will turn back to you. [14]Deliver me from the guilt of bloodshed, O god, you who are God my Savior, and my tongue will sing of your righteousness. [15]Open my lips, Lord, and my mouth will declare your praise. [16]You do not delight in sacrifice, or I would bring it; you do not take pleasure in burnt offerings. [17]My sacrifice, O God, is a broken spirit, a broken and contrite heart you, God, will not despise.

The Psalmist cried out for his sins to be taken away and his heart to be pure. In this Scripture, we see that if the Psalmist's heart were to be pure, songs of righteousness, praises to God, and ministering to those who were sinners would come forth out of his mouth. These things are important. If we desire to follow Jesus Christ, what we allow to enter our heart through our eyes and ears must be those things which are pure. In doing so, out of our mouth will flow those things which will glorify God. As we pour out of our mouth that which is good, it will touch lives to set captives free. It will touch lives that people turn back to God, and it will take brokenness many times to bring us back to God. If others are not willing to lay their lives at the cross to follow God, who will be the messengers to take those bold messages that will set people free and bring them back to God? God desires that we are broken in order that our heart is right. He does not desire sacrifice but brokenness. Without a right heart, people cannot walk in an intimate relationship with Him. However, it will be through the brokenness that we make the choice to let go of this world, lay our lives at the cross and follow Him.

Brokenness normally happens in the midst of a storm. It is through those storms where our lives radically change and where our relationship with our Creator takes form. This is where I teach often to be thankful for our storms. Without a storm, we would never even seek God. Without a storm, our relationship with God would probably suffer. Remember, relationship is the key to salvation. The word salvation is not to just be thrown about lightly. It is more than a word. Salvation is a change of life, a heart change! As we seek God, we find Him! The Scriptures tell us to seek and we will find. We find God; we find the Holly Spirit, and we find the Word which is Jesus Christ. God's Word is living and is life to those who find it! As we find Jesus, He comes alive within us. As we find Him, we fall madly in love with Him. Jesus said, *"If you love me...!"*

John 14:15 (ESV) "If you love me, you will keep my commandments."

John 14:23 (ESV) Jesus answered him, "If anyone loves me, he will keep my word..."

Jesus goes on to say in John 21 that if we love Him we will feed His lambs and His sheep and tend to them. Love is a powerful tool. When we love like God loves, it radically changes lives. Loving from the inside is all about loving like God loves, loving like Jesus Christ. Jesus shares with us that if we are loving from the inside, we will have the desire to keep His commandments and walk according to the Word of God. Our purpose in this life will be all about people because we will be operating in the God-kind of love. We may think we can walk this life out merely by the world kind of love and the majority try to do just that; however, we will lack in all areas of our life because we were created to love like God. Without love, we are nothing and have nothing. God being the definition of love means that without Him, the love you have or the love you feel is merely a superficial love and eventually it will fade or go away. Even our love we have for our children at some point will not be enough to radically change circumstances. Relationships today are only strengthened through Jesus Christ. Our salvation through Christ is only secure when that relationship is intact. As we seek and find Him, everything about Him goes with this life. Salvation through Him becomes a way of life. Our life's focus becomes for people but that is because His Word infiltrates through our blood and our walk becomes finding and remaining on that narrow pathway that few find. We may think that it is not possible to obey His commandments but that is only because our heart is not right. Once we are striving to be closer to Him, that pathway becomes easier and like I said, it actually becomes a way of life.

To clarify what our life should look like, we can go back to the first disciples who lived and breathed the Scriptures. In doing this, we see men and women that sold out to God by daily striving to get the gospel of Jesus Christ to the world. Treading through the storms, the trials, the tests and the persecution, they remained standing to the end. They never compromised, and they did not go back to their prior lives. Following Jesus Christ means knowing that when you miss it, you make it right. When you miss it, you go to the Father for forgiveness and strength that you do not continue fulfilling those strongholds which will ultimately bring you to an end minus God.

All the commandments which we should strive to live out through Him go back to Exodus but also to the New Testament. In Exodus, most people are aware of these commandments:

- You shall have no other gods before me
- You shall not make for yourself a carved image
- You shall not take the name of the Lord your God in vain
- Remember the Sabbath day to keep it holy
- Honor your father and your mother
- You shall not murder
- You shall not commit adultery

- You shall not steal
- You shall not bear false witness against your neighbor
- You shall not covet

Many are not aware that Jesus added to the commandments in Exodus, saying:

- Love one another as I have loved you *(John 13:34)*
- Go into all the world and preach the gospels to all *(Mark 16:15)*

However, realize that we are not capable of doing all that we are commanded through our own strength. For us to be able to love on the inside, we must allow the Holy Spirit access into our lives that we draw strength with the presence of God living inside of us.

Not too long ago, as I was seeking God in my prayer time, I remember being in a place where I was struggling in areas due to the storm I was facing. As I cried out to God, He spoke to me. This was the brilliant wisdom I was given, *"Stop looking at the storm as being so immense that you feel overwhelmed, just simply say every day as often as need be, 'Today, I choose love.'"*

As I thought about this, I realized when we choose love, are we not choosing God? God is love; He is the very definition of love. So, when I felt overwhelmed, I was simply to say, *"Lord today, I just choose love!"* I thought to myself, this was too simple, but I proceeded and said, *"Lord, today I choose love, whatever that means, I just choose love right now!"* Think about this long and hard. We can choose to do whatever we are feeling at the time or we can just simply choose love. As I spoke those words, I had also said, *"Whatever that means Lord!"* As I began to think about this, I felt silly that I had spoken to God, whatever that means. Did I not know what that meant? All was good because He replied to me, *"Yes, whatever that means – think about that!"* I did, I thought about what came out of my mouth. No, I didn't really know what that meant. I can say the words all day long that I choose love, but did I really know what that looked like? As I thought about it, I realized that my words spoken were exactly what I needed to say. Let me explain, you are in a storm and in any storm, it is hard to see clearly. This is the first reason we must take our eyes off the storm and choose God or choose love which is the same thing. The second thing we must do is pause. Yes, we pause to think about what that means. Every storm is different and depending on your storm, the way you choose love will also be different. So, I realized that *"whatever that means"* is the perfect timing to pause. Many times, in the book of Psalms you will see *"Selah."* There have been many who have tried to explain what *"Selah"* means with many theories. With Psalms being songs, many believed the Selah to be a pause or a break in music or to measure the weight of the music. The best explanation I came upon was that Selah meant to carefully weigh the meaning of what you just read. I believe that God is a God that knows His people will perish from lack of knowledge because we do not step back enough to take in what we just read to make sure we are understanding. I think that when we are in the midst of our storms, we must take that pause to say, *"Lord, whatever that means in this particular storm, I choose love."* Maybe in our pause, we will think about the storm and think about how we have tried to handle the storm in the natural producing undesirable results. Maybe in our pause we will think about how love would look in this situation. Maybe in our pause we would realize that choosing love right now may change our actions. Maybe we would remain silent instead of overreacting. Maybe we would speak something nice instead of something we would regret later. Maybe we would respond to someone in a positive way instead of a negative way. I don't know about you, but just saying the words, *"Lord, I choose love right now,"* brings added peace to my life and a love that feels purer than any love in this world. However, what if we took the time to reflect on the situation where it's not about just saying the words but what we do next will be the key to learning just how to love in the storms. Maybe this is why there is so much emphasis about love in the Word of God. Are we not told that everything will pass away but 3 things, faith, hope, and love – with the greatest of these being love!

1 Corinthians 13:1-13 (ESV) The Way of Love
[1] If I speak in the tongues of men and of angels, but have not love, I am a noisy gong or a clanging cymbal. [2] And if I have prophetic powers, and understand all mysteries and all knowledge, and if I have all faith, so as to remove mountains, but have not love, I am nothing. [3] If I give away all I have, and if I deliver up my body to be burned, but have not love, I gain nothing. [4] Love is patient and kind; love does not envy or boast; it is not arrogant [5] or rude. It does not insist on its own way; it is not irritable or resentful; [6] it does not rejoice at wrongdoing, but rejoices with the truth. [7] Love bears all things, believes all things, hopes all things, endures all things. [8] Love never ends. As for prophecies, they will pass away; as for tongues, they will cease; as for

knowledge, it will pass away. ⁹ For we know in part and we prophesy in part, ¹⁰ but when the perfect comes, the partial will pass away. ¹¹ When I was a child, I spoke like a child, I thought like a child, I reasoned like a child. When I became a man, I gave up childish ways. ¹² For now we see in a mirror dimly, but then face to face. Now I know in part; then I shall know fully, even as I have been fully known. ¹³ So now faith, hope, and love abide, these three; but the greatest of these is love.

CHAPTER FIVE
I CAN'T MAKE YOU LOVE HIM

As I shared in the introduction, this book was inspired due to my granddaughter several years ago. To go a little deeper, my granddaughter has lived with me her whole life. For a large part of her life, I was very involved with the church where we spent almost 7 days a week within the church building. Her friends were all raised in Christian homes but none of them were in her school she attended at that time. Being in the public schools, she was different than most in her class. She had no friends in the public schools during those days and was singled out by many where she was bullied. At that time, I can remember praying, *"Lord, she spends every day of the week learning of you only to be sent in among wolves trying to devour her."* I felt as though I was giving her a life where she would know Jesus intimately and then sending her out 5 days a week into the battlefield alone as a little girl to test her faith. She was too young, and I felt that something had to change. This change began one particular day as I shared earlier. It was easy to see that she did not want any part of praying to a God that was allowing her to be subject to the harsh reality of this world for 5 days a week. Where was God anyway? Why would He allow her to go through what she was having to endure at such a young age? I could tell that she was steadily drifting away from God. You could tell that in her pain of not wanting to go to school, she did not believe that God really cared. It was easy to see the look on her face was one that said, *"God, if you are real, why do I not see you in the midst of my pain trying to help deliver me from my enemies?"* Isn't this what most of us feel when we are in a particular situation where it appears everything and everyone is against us and we wonder, *"God, where are you?"* It was that particular morning that God showed me that I could not make her love Him because I couldn't even make myself love Him. However, I knew if she grew up and did not fall in love with God, with Jesus Christ, she would never make it to Heaven. Isn't that true for all of us? We take one day at a time, struggle in this life, pain comes, suffering comes, and then we cry out to a God that we are supposed to believe in for answers. *"God, where are you?" "God, don't you love me anymore?"* That day began to change the way I looked at things and I hope it will do the same for you.

As we begin to think about this, we can see that we are not capable of making ourselves fall in love with anyone. We can grow to love people, but love is not something that we can just make happen. So, where do we go from here? Jesus said, *"If you love me you will feed my sheep and my lambs!"* If we are not doing those things, is it because we do not love Him?

I can teach you, instruct you, and train you because the Holy Spirit is my teacher, and He reminds me of all truths. I can tell you how much I love Jesus. I can tell you everything that He has done for my life and my family, but I CAN'T MAKE <u>YOU</u> LOVE HIM no matter how hard I try! With me, it was about reading my love letter aloud to Him. With my daughter, it was about singing her love letter to Him. However, in reality these things are not what will make you fall in love with Him. This was only a method of homework to help develop a relationship. Sometimes our relationships need help and the simple little methods that are used with marriage counselors to strengthen a relationship are only developed for us to pause. What that means is that we become so distracted by the things in this world which is not by accident, and these things become our gods. satan has a plan too, and his plan is to make sure that we do not seek for God to that intimate level. If all this technology must happen for prophesy to be filled, part of that prophesy is that the *"many"* will stand before God and be turned away from Heaven because He tells us that they never knew Him. It is the relationship that matters, and any relationship takes time, patience, understanding, strength, and I could go on and on. It is about investment. We will always invest in those things we relish, such as sports, automobiles, boats, etc.; however, many of us never take the time out to invest in the only thing that will secure our life eternal. In fact, many of us do not even invest in our own children or our spouse, and these relationships also suffer. However, a relationship with God will never be some kind of a formula that will change your heart. It is not works that will ensure your salvation. It is totally about knowing Him, and if it takes you spending the time daily to speak out a love letter to Him or in whatever measure is right for you, then by you doing so - you are pausing your life to get to know Him. As we do this, we will really get to know Him. To know Him is to love Him. You cannot learn of Him and not fall in love with Him. As you fall in love, your heart changes and then your desires will also change in that you will never choose the things in this world over the spiritual or over your family.

Even though I can't make you love Him, I can tell you that if you seek Him diligently, you will fall madly in love with Him and then you will strive to please Him! That's what we do when we really love someone, we desire to make them happy! Your life will change for the better because you will walk with the God-kind of love within you, not with the love that this world knows. It is an unconditional love, but it will cost you everything and then you will gain everything!

As we spend that time to seek God intimately, what we begin to feel for Him will be heartfelt. You will never get to heaven based on words alone because words alone are meaningless when it is not heartfelt. With any relationship, we love to hear the words said to us, but we never believe them when the actions of someone says something totally different. When those we love tell us that they love us, it really means nothing to us if they lie to us, cheat on us, and never have time to spend with us. The same with God, He desires that what we are feeling for Him will be heartfelt. When our words mean something, our actions will also show it. Our actions to God will be where we love spending that intimate time with Him. When we fall in love with God it will bother us extremely when we live a lie, when we cheat, when we go against everything He stands for. Think about it. When we are in love with someone, we want them to be open and honest with us. We want them to be loyal, and we want their time. We want them sharing their life from the ups and downs to the joys and triumphs. Why would God not want the same from us? Are we not created by Him to be like Him? I take this to mean that we desire to be loved because God also desires to be loved.

As the Holy Spirit becomes our teacher and counselor, it will be through Him that we are able to grow in that God-kind of love. It will be through the Holy Spirit that we gain the strength to endure any and everything and travel that narrow road which is not only hard to find but rough to travel. We can do all things through Jesus

Christ, and Jesus left us with the Holy Spirit to guide us in this life. We can and will learn to love with a pure heart that has been transformed as we seek God deeply. A pure heart is minus sin but not minus God!

CHAPTER SIX
HAVING DONE ALL - STAND

Times are tough, and they just keep getting tougher but to those who love Him, they will endure. When faced with the opposition, as true Christians, we hold on. In other words, no matter how fierce the storm, we stand and trust. Paul said it like this in Ephesians:

Ephesians 6:13 (ESV) [13]Therefore take up the whole armor of God, that you may be able to withstand in the evil day, and having done all, to stand firm.

There are times that we try to calm the storms by using natural means, and it seems as if the storm just gets bigger until it is out of our control. It is during these times, we must realize that God did not call us to fix the storms by natural means. In fact, God never called us to even face the storms alone. When we have done all that we can do, it is time to stand. I remember a particular storm a while back and how I struggled with going back and forth from trying to find measures to fix the storm and then trying to stand while waiting on God. I remember I would hear the voice say, *"You have not done this yet,"* and I would go and try something different. I would hear the voice say, *"You need to wait on the Lord,"* so I would stop and give it to God once again. Then when I would hear the voice with an idea of what I could do, I would say, *"No, I'm just waiting on the Lord."* However, there were times that daily I would hear the voice telling me to do this one thing I had not done yet. I kept saying *"no"* because I had made the decision to just stand and wait on God. I felt like it was not God's voice but when the voice continued daily, I felt frustrated and there was no peace. I was riding my bike one day and expressed what I was feeling to God. I didn't want to miss God, but I didn't want to keep doing things in myself instead of patiently waiting on Him either. As I talked with God about how I was not sure if it was His voice or maybe my own voice wanting to continue doing something I had not tried yet to perhaps change the situation. On this particular day, God gave me a Scripture. That Scripture was one that I teach so often but when you are actually in the storm, many times you cannot comprehend that your answer was always embedded in your heart. That Scripture is Ephesians 6:13 which began this chapter. Having done all, then you stand! God asked me, *"Have you done all that you know to do?"* You see, God meets us half way, but He expects us to follow through with what we are taught to do according to His Word. I had not done all I knew to do myself and that was why I was frustrated and had no peace. Therefore, I kept having the thought come to me on something I had not done. Here is what He means by this, in any battle whether spiritual or natural, we do everything we can do in ourselves and then we let it go and give it to God. At that place is where we stand. Doing all you know to do is not going to fix the storm because it is never about fixing any storm, it is about allowing the end result of that storm to be what God intended. God allows the storms in life in order to radically change people's hearts. We should never want storms to end until they have done what was intended in order that lives are radically changed. Once we have done all that we know to do in the natural, it may seem that the things we did resulted in nothing being changed, but we must remember that many times the things we do will plant seeds that God can cultivate once we stand. Through that cultivation process the change occurs being God's will not our own. We must understand that the end result will be God's plan not necessarily what we had contemplated in our own minds. This is the difficult part because one storm I have faced for several years has not played out to the end. I know what the outcome could be in a couple of different scenarios, and of course, one of those outcomes would be what my heart would want but the other scenario could very well be what God was planning all along. God will always prepare us for the different scenarios in order that we can see why the end result may not be what we wanted. Once we accept this in our heart as being God's plan, then we can trust Him that there was a reason. Once I got through the difficult part of doing all I could do, and I let go giving it to God, I stepped back so that He could take the wheel. Once you let go knowing you have done your part, your peace will come. Today, my peace remains over my storm because I understand what the scenarios could be, but the ultimate plan will be in His timing not mine. If we truly know God and trust Him, the end result will never really matter because we also understand that the way we think, our thoughts are not God's thoughts. Our ways are not God's ways and if we really know Him to be the Creator of all, we also know how much He loves those who belong to Him. At this place, we understand that the end result will always be what was best for ourselves and all those we love.

Let me clarify that doing all you know to do is not insinuating that God wants us to do what we know to do when it does not line up with living a holy life. The thought which came to me was not to do something which was going to be selfish on my part to benefit me in anyway. Please do not take this to mean that it is okay for you to do anything which breaks the Ten

Commandments or the command which Jesus gave for us to love one another because going against any commandment does not give glory to God. satan will definitely give you thoughts on how to handle storms which are not godly thoughts and those things are not what God is referring to doing all YOU know to do in a situation. It is not okay to take situations in your own hands and act out violently with other people. It is not okay to say ugly harsh things to people for whatever reason. It is not okay to turn your back on others because of whatever has transpired in a relationship all the while hoping that they will pay for anything they have done. We must remember that Jesus gave us the new commandment to love others as He has loved us. Breaking any commandment is NOT planting the right seeds for God to cultivate and when we walk in hate towards others, we stop our own prayers and we stop God working on our own behalf.

Matthew 6:15 (ESV) [15]but if you do not forgive others their trespasses, neither will your Father forgive your trespasses.

Proverbs 28:9 (NKJV) [9]One who turns away his ear from hearing the law, even his prayer is an abomination.

Mark 11:25 (ESV) [25]And whenever you stand praying, forgive, if you have anything against anyone, so that your Father also who is in heaven may forgive you your trespasses."

1 Corinthians 13:1-3 (ESV) [1]If I speak in the tongues of men and of angels, but have not love, I am a noisy gong or a clanging cymbal. [2]And if I have prophetic powers, and understand all mysteries and all knowledge, and if I have all faith, so as to remove mountains, but have not love, I am nothing. ³If I give away all I have, and if I deliver up my body to be burned, but have not love, I gain nothing.

Now, just because we are to love does not mean we are to accept situations or actions of others which are totally contrary to the Word of God. We just plant the seeds and step back to allow God to cultivate. We may be at a place where we must stop associating with people we love for a timeframe. This is all good because sometimes this is necessary for God to be able to cultivate. We must just always know that as true Christians, we pray for those who persecute us because we may have been at that same place as they are at one time in our own life prior to Jesus Christ.

Letting go of the circumstances once we have done all and trusting God is our place where we stand. This is where we let go of the circumstance by giving it to God. We say, *"God, I have done all I know to do, this is Your storm and I trust You to fight this battle for me!"* I have been at this place more than once, but it is all about trusting Him. When we let go of the circumstances, we are holding on to God and trusting in Him. Letting go and holding on is walking in that God-kind of faith. Faith lets go of the storms and faith holds on to the very substance that will grow you to a place where you learn to walk Christ-like. It is all about walking in the God-kind of faith. Faith says, *"I will trust you in the storm!"* If we are really trusting Him, there will be some changes. We need to ask ourselves these questions:

1) Am I still worrying about this situation?
2) Am I still living in fear over this situation?

3) Is this situation still consuming my thoughts?

If you answer yes to any of these questions, you have not given that storm to God. He taught me this many years ago. When I realized that I was still holding on to the storm even though my words were saying, *"God, I give it to you,"* I really had not given it to Him. At that point, I cried out, *"God, show me how to let it go and give it to you!"* It's not that we don't want to give it to God, but it is a matter of not knowing how to let it go. The changes that had to occur within me was about learning how to not allow the circumstances to consume my mind. God showed me that my focus needed to be on what He called me to do. In my case, it began with opening my home for a women's group that I began to minister to in those days. It also was about me studying to gain greater wisdom and knowledge of God and begin pouring His revelation into what would later be these books. At one point, I was ministering to the prisons, pouring into girls that would cross my path, a ministry within my home, going into other homes to pray for families, and any other place He would send me. After a while, I realized that my life was so consumed with the ministry that those storms that had once plagued me were no longer important and what plagued my mind was the Word of God. There is healing in His Word. There is peace in His Word. There is joy in His Word. If you desire that healing, peace and joy, it begins with filling yourself with more of Him. His joy will overflow from you when you are filled with Him.

John 7:37-38 (ESV) [37]On the last day of the feast, the great day, Jesus stood up and cried out, "If anyone thirsts, let him come to me and drink. [38]Whoever believes in me, as the Scripture has said, 'Out of his heart will flow rivers of living water.'"

We only receive from Jesus as we seek Him deeply. Come to Him and He will fill you with life, living water. In that life, there will be an abundance and part of that abundance is joy. Jesus gives us what He has, and it is only through God that we gain real peace, joy, love, etc. If you look at the fruits of the Spirit, you will see that those fruits are love, joy, peace, patience, kindness, goodness, faithfulness, gentleness and self-control. *(Galatians 5:22-23)*

As I was growing in this myself, those storms had subsided but none of it really seemed that important anymore. I realized that as I spent more time pouring into the Word of God, I was learning to trust and walk by faith. Here is the thing, it does not matter how much you worry and fear over a situation, your worry and fear will not change anything. However, God can change your circumstances when you learn to walk in faith. Walking in faith begins by trusting and standing on His Word. In the midst of the storm, we stand!

As I was following Jesus in the path God had chosen for my life, I had become so consumed with the ministry He had placed in my heart, that my thoughts were no longer consumed with the storm. This is letting go of the storm, no longer holding on to it and merely standing! This was how I learned to let go! Letting go will automatically happen when our thoughts and our walk is consumed with Jesus Christ. When our daily walk is filled with doing those things He has called us to do, there will be no room for worry or fear over whatever storm you are facing. You do all you know to do in the natural, and then you get back up because you will feel as though you have been knocked down. You brush yourself off and as a Christian, you step forth for whatever assignment God has called you to. Any assignment will always be built around people. We are all called to *"go"* and share Jesus. We are all called to be the *"John the Baptists"* of this world preparing for the second coming of Jesus Christ. This happens by filling your heart with His Word, pouring into Him by seeking Him alone.

All of this goes back to your eyes and ears. We guard them by what we choose to watch, read, and listen to. We all know that one day, this world as we know it will fade away. You will know that prophecy is continually being fulfilled as you watch for the signs which are coming to pass at an alarming rate all over this world. The time and harvest is ripe, but the laborers remain few. The day is here to prepare for the second coming of Jesus Christ, and if the Christian community would rise to be the *"John the Baptists"* of this generation, there would be little time for worry and fear. If we would rise to be what we were called to be, there would be more time to grow in faith and grow in those things of God that will ultimately bring glory unto His name. We should be looking forward to the day that we stand before God knowing if we have done all we know to do in this world, He will tell us, *"Well done my faithful servant!"*

CHAPTER SEVEN
PIONEERS FOR CHRIST

What exactly is a pioneer? Years ago, when I stepped out to go in a different direction than those I had been associating with in the Christian community, I realized that most people were accustomed to remaining with what was familiar to them. People become accustomed to going through the same motions week after week in all facets of their lives. They become accustomed to their same lifestyles, working, playing, and even worshiping God. We become indoctrinated in a certain ministry and week after week our service to God basically is grounded or established in the same manner as those we have chosen to associate with, those same circle of Christian friends. To be more specific, whatever denomination we choose to engage in, the way we serve God remains the same as those walking that same path each week beside us and it becomes stale – there are no changes! Most people do not like change. The majority of people today become accustomed to doing things a certain way. Change always hurts, but change is necessary if we want to serve God the way His Word teaches. You see, God never changes; He has remained the same over time. *(Malachi 3:6)* However, man has always walked away from God and His teachings because walking with God requires letting go of ourselves. We are a selfish people that do not want to lay our lives down to serve anyone, but if we truly desire a relationship with our Creator, it will take just that. We must make the change to serve a God that does not change, and this will take running this race alone many times. The majority WILL NOT follow a God that requires too much from them. The majority WILL NOT give up their own selfish ways that they have become accustomed to. The majority WILL NOT even consider that their ways may not be the right way.

Haggai 1:5-7 (ESV) ⁵Now, therefore, thus says the Lord of hosts: Consider your ways. ⁶You have sown much, and harvested little. You eat, but you never have enough; you drink, but you never have your fill. You clothe yourselves, but no one is warm. And he who earns wages does so to put them into a bag with holes. ⁷"Thus says the Lord of hosts: Consider your ways.

To consider that our ways may not be the right way would take too much of our time away from what we desire to do in order to seek a God that never changes. The majority would much rather find or create a god to serve that can be taught once or twice a week from a pulpit and leave feeling as though all is well so that they can continue in their selfish lifestyles. Many people walk away from the church because after some time, their relationship with God seems distant. I have always been one that questioned the methods and motives within the church building. I have been one that always wanted to seek God to a degree that was not happening within the church. I have always been one that would step out and take a chance on doing something different only to be chastised by man. My personality has always been one that chose not to follow the crowd but to wander out in the desert alone if need be in order to find something different. There have always been times in my life of uncertainty, yet even though those areas were unknown, it drove me to seek deeper instead of being afraid. I have encountered situations which produced fear but have had to turn to God to trust and continue to wade through those waters not knowing what lay ahead. I would have been considered a rebel during my teens and 20s because if I believed in something, I fought for that cause. God needs rebels today but those who are willing to fight for His cause and not their own. My point is that a rebel personality is someone unafraid of what may lay ahead all the while plowing forward for a particular cause.

Like a rebel, a pioneer is one who is also unafraid of plowing forward into territories unknown. A pioneer will venture into unknown territories and will also open new areas of thought. Years ago, pioneers were those who led the way for others to follow. Think about it, if there were not people willing to wander into territories which were unknown, America would have never been discovered. However, God had a plan for America and there were those who chose to go forth even though it was uncertain the outcome. If you study Christopher Columbus, you will learn that he heard the voice of the Holy Spirit many times. Columbus was a man of God and was chosen by God to find the new world. Although he was persecuted many times and was believed to be a man rambling on about things which were not understood, he made the decision to continue in the walk which he felt was ordained by God. Columbus spent much time studying the Word of God and knew the Bible as well as he knew the sea. Of course, he gave all the credit to God. Columbus was not an educated man, yet his skills in language, cosmography, and nautical science were highly competent.[1] At sea, Columbus believed that God not only gave him the necessary skills to carry out the plan He had for him, but he also believed that God had His hands upon his life and was leading him to a new world which he ultimately found. In doing so, he believed that

God was protecting him through every storm and encounter they came upon, and God did! Columbus expressed many times that the Holy Spirit had spoken to him regarding his destination. However, the majority thought his ramblings to be just that. Just like today, we do not always listen to those messages where someone claims that God or the Holy Spirit has spoken to them. Luckily, there are many writings which have been preserved that Columbus wrote himself. Today, we can understand that God did have a purpose for America and that someone had to discover it. Yes, it is okay to give the credit to God for leading that someone to discover the new world. God is the same today as He was yesterday, and He still speaks to those who seek Him diligently. From Columbus' writings and from those who knew him well, writing about his voyages and experiences, we can see that God was very much a part of this man's life. If you read any of these writings, you will find a man who had unshakable faith and believed he was an instrument of God's hands. His words as written in one such document which Columbus gave credit to God said, *"He bestowed the arts of seamanship upon me in abundance, and has given me what was necessary from astronomy, geometry, and arithmetic; and has given me adequate inventiveness in my soul, encouraging me to go forward, and without ceasing they inflame me with a sense of urgency."*[2] To those who do not believe, Columbus' words may have seemed to be ramblings but to those who do believe, it is because they have had similar experiences. Those who seek God intimately as Columbus did, they know that God is the same today as He was yesterday. They know that He pours out His Spirit upon all who seek after Him. Columbus was a pioneer and unafraid to venture into areas unknown and because of his obedience to a God we cannot see in the natural sense, America was discovered. Columbus gave his life for the purpose that God ordained him. Columbus' years were spent running his own personal race towards the mark that God called him to. As Christians, we are to be like Columbus even though there will be those who think we are crazy. Even though we may not fully understand why God is leading us into a direction unknown, in our spirit we will trust. By faith, we trust in a God we cannot see in the natural, but we definitely hear His voice in the spiritual. In a few other writings of Columbus, he stated, *"God made me the messenger of the new heaven and new earth, of which He spoke in the Apocalypse of St. John after having spoken of it by the mouth of Isaiah, and he showed me where to find it."*[3] *"I could sense his hand upon me, so that it became clear to me that it was feasible to navigate from here to the Indies, and he gave me the will to do it."*[4] Although Columbus thought that he was searching to locate the Indies, God had another plan and that plan was fulfilled. In Columbus' mind, he desired to find the route to the Indies and that was okay because it caused him to take that step forward so God could do something miraculous. It did not matter that what Columbus desired was different than what God had planned, what mattered was that God needed a messenger to be willing to go. We do not always have to know exactly what God is doing, we just have to be obedient to that calling. Also, as I was reading Columbus' writings about how he sensed God's hand upon him, it made me think about a time that I also felt God's hand literally on me. I'm not going to go into deep detail, but many years ago, our home caught on fire in the middle of the night while we were all sleeping. At the start of the fire, I was awoken because of God's hand literally placed upon my back as He pushed me into a sitting position in the bed. I did not even know there was a fire and didn't know why I was sitting upright in the bed. As I began to lay back down, I felt His hand once again lift me up. I knew then that God wanted me to get up for some reason. As I climbed out of the bed being obedient, I discovered that smoke was beginning to pour into our bathroom. We were saved along with our home because God is still the same God of miracles today as He was yesterday. It only takes having that mentality of a pioneer, one who knows there are things still to discover and willing to take that step forward all the while trusting in God.

In my studies, I also discovered that Christopher Columbus wrote a book on prophesies. In those days and at that time period, people thought that those things he shared from the Holy Spirit were not of God. Is that not how the world views people today which sell out for God and plow forward unstoppable into the unknown? Yes, Columbus was a pioneer unafraid of the mission God had placed ahead of him and unstoppable even though others considered him foolish and persecuted him severely.

Pioneers for Christ have always been present. John the Baptist was a pioneer preparing the way for Jesus Christ as he stepped forth unafraid of the unknown.

Matthew 11:7-19 (ESV) ⁷As they went away, Jesus began to speak to the crowds concerning John: "What did you go out into the wilderness to see? A reed shaken by the wind? ⁸What then did you go out to see? A man dressed in soft clothing? Behold, those who wear soft clothing are in kings' houses. ⁹What then did you go out to see? A prophet? Yes, I tell you, and more than a prophet. ¹⁰This is he of whom it is written, "'Behold, I send my messenger before your face, who will prepare your way before you.' ¹¹Truly, I say to you, among those born of women there has arisen no one greater than John the Baptist. Yet the one who is least in the kingdom of heaven is greater than he. ¹²From the days of John the Baptist until now the kingdom of heaven has suffered violence, and the violent take it by force. ¹³For all the Prophets and the Law prophesied until John, ¹⁴and if you are willing to accept it, he is Elijah who is to come. ¹⁵He who has ears to hear, let him hear. ¹⁶"But to what shall I compare this generation? It is like children sitting in the marketplaces and calling to their playmates, ¹⁷"'We played the flute for you, and you did not dance; we sang a dirge, and you did not mourn.' ¹⁸For John came neither eating nor drinking, and they say, 'He has a demon.' ¹⁹The Son of Man came eating and drinking, and they say, 'Look at him! A glutton and a drunkard, a friend of tax collectors and sinners!' Yet wisdom is justified by her deeds."

John was a pioneer, he had a pioneering spirit. He was unafraid of what man could do to him because he was on a mission – one mission and that was to prepare the way for the coming of Jesus Christ. The church was created for one purpose. That purpose was to go and make disciples for Jesus Christ in order that we prepare ourselves and others for His second coming. This would be the Great Commission!

Matthew 28:18-20 (NKJV) ¹⁸And Jesus came and spoke to them, saying, "All Authority has been given to Me in heaven and on earth. ¹⁹Go therefore and make disciples of all the nations, baptizing them in the name of the Father and of the Son and of the Holy Spirit,

[20]teaching them to observe all things that I have commanded you; and lo, I am with you always, even to the end of the age." Amen.

What exactly is a commission? The word commission is an official charge given to a group of people or a command. Meaning, if you consider yourself a Christian, which is a follower of Jesus Christ, then you are part of this group of people. Jesus gave all those who are following Him the command to go and make disciples. Therefore, we are all called to be pioneers. We were never called to become complacent remaining in one place going through the same motions week after week and calling it Christianity. The church has received a bad name over the years because it has been conformed to this world instead of being transformed by the Word of God through the Holy Spirit. I have always questioned the motives of how one man can be over a body of believers *(that man not being Jesus Christ)* and conduct his church service in a way to please the congregation. To emphasize, I have been in churches where the pastor would sugar coat the message in order that the majority would not leave because then there would not be enough funds coming in to pay the bills. Then there are many of the churches that have their programs where they allow 15 minutes for this, 10 minutes for that, 20 minutes for a message and let's not forget to give Jesus time to save and heal people, so they allow 15 minutes for the organized healing and salvation rituals, in order to get the people out by noon or they will not come back. Or, at least you must end the service where those needing to leave by noon can feel free to do so. Over the last decade or so, the church has also become a place to satisfy the people with their many programs, entertainment, social gatherings and let's not forget the coffee shops. Why do we really go to church? I ask this because when I stepped away from a church that had it all because God was leading me into uncertain waters which felt totally uncomfortable to my flesh, my first response in the churches I visited was, *"Lord, where are the children's programs and the music (entertainment)?"* My flesh was totally dissatisfied because I had become accustomed to man's methods of driving in the multitudes in order to keep them satisfied where they would not leave. I will never forget God asking me, *"Why do you come to church?"* Do we go to church to fellowship with others? Yes, we are to be joined together with other believers, but if we are really joined with other believers, our walk with Jesus Christ will look like the walk of those disciples many years ago. So, once again, why do we go to church? For the fellowship, for the entertainment? I mean even many pastors from the pulpits entertain the multitudes each week with jokes. I suppose jokes are not a bad thing, but I haven't been able to find any sermons from Jesus or His followers in the Bible where they began a sermon with a joke in order to capture their audience's attention to gain the multitudes. Also, I kind of look at salvation as being something very serious not a joke. Are we looking for a church that has it all, entertainment, concerts, comedy hour, computer kiosks for our children's entertainment that we can capture the young people? Are we looking for a place that has social gatherings, book stores where they make more profit besides the tithe, and even grocery stores to make it easier for their congregation to grab a gallon of milk and loaf of bread before heading home? Also, in traveling this year to another state, I discovered there is a mega-church that now owns their own neighborhoods of nice homes where their followers can buy their homes and live among the other members, so they can be surrounded Monday through Sunday with the same followers. Yes, I have seen far too much which sickens me and probably many things I have yet to see that is out there. I remember loving the coffee shop and then I found myself at a small church minus all the things I loved, but the messages were not sugar coated and it was exactly where I needed to be at that time. Do we want to follow the multitudes on that wide pathway or are we really looking for that narrow pathway? Jesus said that few would even find the narrow pathway. *(Matthew 7:13-14)* Why is that? I will tell you why, it is because most people who claim to be Christians are conformed to the religion which man has created with all its entertainment through the music, the jokes, the socializing among the congregations, etc. There is something to entertain everyone who attends. I must look back to the ministry of Jesus Christ and John the Baptist. Both ministries were one and the same. They spoke out to the people with bold messages that we do not want to hear but we need to hear; otherwise, we will never find that narrow pathway and one day as we stand before God, He will say, *"Depart from me!"* You can spend your whole life trying to conform to man's modern-day Christianity, or you can venture out to seek God to a deeper degree where the relationship is between you and God. Do you really know Him?

A pioneering spirit should begin with those who are seasoned followers of Jesus Christ, meaning those who have laid their lives down and picked up their cross to follow Jesus. Pioneers for Christ are those who have walked away from what feels comfortable to their flesh in order to seek Him deeper. They are those who continually pour into the Word of God in order to KNOW

HIM to a greater degree, and they are those who hear the voice of the Shepherd and follow Him even when it means they may have to let go of their own desires in this life such as sports, television, etc.

What does the lifestyle of a pioneer look like? I spent a lot of time watching Little House on the Prairie with my granddaughter because it was a clean family oriented show. Many times, God leads me to watch things from time to time because I learn valuable lessons. In watching this series, which basically portrayed the life of a pioneer prior to all the comforts we have in America today, I was able to see that their lives were simple and focused on the family and Christianity. This was a time in America where many people lived a very simple life minus comforts, and they were happy. Today, we have a hard time being happy without the comforts or entertainment. I have met young people that were bored if they were not doing something every night for entertainment. I think it is good for us to look back to a time when there was no entertainment. A time when things were simple. A time when the family unit was important. A time when God was the center of the family unit. A time when gathering around on the front porch after supper to sing gospel hymns and read the Bible was part of their lives. A time when the family raised their children by godly-principles not expecting the schools and the churches to do that for them. A time when entertainment for their children was not sitting them in front of a television or computer but a time when families gathered together for picnics in the fields and at the ponds. When dads taught their children how to fish and hunt instead of allowing their children to become street smart where they could learn to make money by selling drugs and living a life of crime. A time when dads were very much a part of raising their children and being the head over their household. I'm not saying that all families in those days were doing everything right, but what I am saying is that we have entered a time where our lifestyles have changed so drastically from those days. The days we live in today have become so fast paced where daily, we are running a race, but it is not the race Paul spoke of. We are running to keep up with our neighbors and our friends. We want what everyone else has. We want the best of everything. We want the big house and nice cars. We want beautiful furniture and money in the bank. We want elaborate vacations. We want the latest gadgets whether it be electronics, appliances, etc. We want what everyone else has and this includes the biggest and most vibrant churches to worship God. However, these things have become distractions which separate us from God. We feel satisfied with where our lives have taken us, and this satisfaction keeps us from seeking deeper for the secrets of God.

Matthew 13:10-13(ESV) ¹⁰Then the disciples came and said to him, "Why do you speak to them in parables?" ¹¹And he answered them, "<u>To you it has been given to know the secrets of the kingdom of heaven</u>, but to them it has not been given. ¹²For to the one who has, more will be given, and he will have an abundance, but from the one who has not, even what he has will be taken away. ¹³This is why I speak to them in parables, because seeing they do not see, and hearing they do not hear, nor do they understand.

Jesus is NOT speaking of having more of the luxuries we see all around us. If that is what you believe, you have eyes to see but you are not seeing, and you have ears to hear but you are not hearing.

Romans 12:2 (NKJV) ²And do not be conformed to this world, but be transformed by the renewing of your mind, that you may prove what is that good and acceptable and perfect will of God.

A pioneer for Jesus Christ will never be satisfied with man's methods because in their spirit they will always feel that there is something more and there is something different. A pioneering spirit will always question that which seems like light and that which seems as darkness. I remember when my granddaughter had to do a report on an autobiography and she chose the Little House on the Prairie autobiography by Laura Ingalls. I remember that Laura spoke of how her father moved them around many times because he was always desiring to see what was on down the road. A pioneering spirit never becomes satisfied. A pioneering spirit seeks and searches to see what lays ahead. Jesus said to *"go"* into all the world. I don't believe that means we all get on airplanes or ships where we literally travel to all parts of the world, but if you look back at the first disciples, they did go. They went from place to place where they could walk or take a boat. They did not remain in one place their whole life. I believe to go means just that. If we are walking with God intimately, we will know when the time is to go and where to go. I believe the main thing to see here is that we never become satisfied where we pitch up a tent in a particular church and get lazy. Most people within their churches never do anything for God. They consider going to church once or twice a week and giving their tithes is good enough. I shudder to think if they even have a relationship with God. Giving your tithe and attending a church service each week are nothing more than works.

Ephesians 2:8-9 (ESV) [8]For by grace you have been saved through faith. And this is not your own doing; it is the gift of God, [9]not a result of works, so that no one may boast.

In this one life that we have, God has given us the ability to choose. He will never choose for you. However, our choices in this life should be to choose good over evil, light over darkness, and life not death. If our choices in this life are not choosing Jesus, we are choosing death. Let me emphasize, we know when we choose to do something which is not of God. When we choose darkness, there is no light in us because He is light and will not associate with the darkness in us.

1 John 1:5-7 (ESV) [5]This is the message we have heard from him and proclaim to you, that God is light, and in him is no darkness at all. [6]<u>If we say we have fellowship with him while we walk in darkness, we lie</u> and do not practice the truth. [7]But if we walk in the light, as he is in the light, we have fellowship with one another, and the blood of Jesus his Son cleanses us from all sin.

Please note that we must have fellowship with Him. When we make the decision to walk away from darkness, this does not mean we have chosen light. Both are choices. You can avoid the dark but if you desire to live a life with Jesus, you still must choose that which is light. Fellowship is a choice and it is a relationship. If you do not choose that which is light even though you walked away from darkness, you are merely empty and have chosen nothing. What happens when you are empty because of walking away from darkness?

Matthew 12:43-45 (ESV) 43"When the unclean spirit has gone out of a person, it passes through waterless places seeking rest, but finds none. 44Then it says, 'I will return to my house from which I came.' And when it comes, it finds the house empty, swept, and put in order. 45Then it goes and brings with it seven other spirits more evil than itself, and they enter and dwell there, and the last state of that person is worse than the first. So also will it be with this evil generation."

You see, in order to walk with Jesus and have a relationship, you must choose just that. To be filled where you are no longer empty takes pouring into Him so that He fills you daily. This takes discipline where you spend time daily reading and studying. It takes time where you talk to Him. I probably spend more time talking to Him when I am riding my bike or driving in my car. These are times when I am alone and opportunities to just communicate with Him. Whatever timeframes you have, begin with just talking to Him but in order to know Him, you must seek Him. In seeking, it goes back to the Word of God. If your desire is to be a true disciple of Jesus Christ, you must seek Him to learn of Him through His Word which is freely given to those who hunger for Truth!

CONCLUSION

We only have this one life and in this life, we must live it well according to Scripture. As I have said, I cannot make you love Him but everything you need for this journey is in the Word of God. We are told that if we seek, we will find; if we ask, we will receive, and if we knock, the door will be opened.

Your life should be all about finding God, finding Jesus Christ, and the Holy Spirit which are all One as we too can become One with them! *(John 17:21)* Jesus did not tell us to ask, seek, and knock because nothing would happen. I have been in many storms in my life which have radically changed me. I have been in a place where I knew of God but didn't know Him. I have been in a place where I did not understand Scripture. I have been in dark places where there was worry and fear; however, I challenge anything you may be going through to break down those barriers or walls in your own life and welcome Jesus in. Seek for Him and you will find Him. Allow the Holy Spirit access to your life. Listen and you will hear, look and you will see!

Relationship is the only way to Heaven and it takes you laying down your own life and seeking Him diligently until you find Him. I want to say that prayer is not some kind of formality where you must pray certain ways or in certain places or with other people in order that God hears you. God already hears you and already knows you. God is merely waiting for you to communicate with Him at any time and any place. As you draw closer and you enter His presence, your prayers will become heartfelt prayers which God can see because He is NOT looking outwardly at all the sins you have committed in your lifetime; He is looking at your heart! Thank goodness that God sees what is on the inside of us and not outwardly because many times we may be struggling in areas, but God knows where we really are in our walk as He knows us from the inside. That is how He looked upon David and even though David's sins were great, God saw so much more because He knew his heart. The good thing is that as we draw closer to Him, our struggles will become less in those areas we are weak because our strength will come from Him.

References

Chapter One
Life Minus God

1. What is the American Dream?
http://america.day-dreamer.de/dream.htm

2. The Rights and Freedoms of Americans
www.tep-online.info/laku/usa/rights.htm

Chapter Seven
Pioneers for Christ

1. Columbus to Dona Juana de la Torre, Raccolta di documenti e stud pubblicati della R. Commissione Colombiana, pt. 1, vol. ii; /Scriti di Cristoforo Colombo, ed. Cesare de Lollis (Rome: 1894), p. 82.

2. Ibid., p. 79.

3. Ibid., p. 66.

4. Raccolta, pt. I, vol. ii, p. 79.

www.ingramcontent.com/pod-product-compliance
Lightning Source LLC
Chambersburg PA
CBHW070205100426
42743CB00013B/3057